# Building your Faith to Walk In Spiritual Victory

There are mountains to climb, while walking through
the valley of the shadow of death, fear no evil, for
God is with you. Have Faith and do not doubt, say
to the mountain be removed and be cast into the
sea and it shall be done.

Published by
BookSurge, LLC
5341 Dorchester Rd, Suite 16
North Charleston, SC 29418

ISBN 1-59457-493-6

Additional copies may be purchased:

Contact customer service at customerservice@booksurge.com
Online at www.GlobalBookPublisher.com
www.BookSurge.com
www.GlobalBookPeddler.com or
By calling toll free, 866-308-6235 ext. 20

Author email address: faithbuilderprophetess@saintly.com

## TABLE OF CONTENTS

## DEDICATION

This book is dedicated to my mother, father, sisters, brother, children, grandson and ex-spouse whose inspiration has given me the impulse to move forward in the things God has ordained for my life in this present world.

I would like to give special thanks to my editor, Mr. Timothy Cator for his commitment in the process and birth of this God inspired book that will be a blessing to many people.

I would like to give special thanks to my Aunt, Laverne O'Neal, and the saints at Kossuth Church of God in Christ in St. Louis, Missouri, with presiding Bishop, Robert Strong for their Prayers.

I would like to give Special Thanks to my Spiritual Father in the Faith, Dr. E.G. Shields, Sr. who is the presiding Pastor of Mt. Beulah Missionary Baptist Church, in St. Louis, Mo., and his lovely wife, who gave me the assurance to stand under the call and anointing God has placed upon my life, through his Powerful Ministering and Teaching with Prayer. They are truly loved and an inspiration to the Body of Christ.

With great gratitude, I am thankful to all the enemies God allowed to come into my life. They enabled me to clearly see the things that were of God. The things that were meant for evil, God turned for my good.

I endure the storms in life by continuing to hold fast to the Word of God and I am blessed continually.

Now, I would like to share with all, this dynamic teaching and ministering tool. It is powerful because it carries the Word of God. It is versatile because it can be used in many ways. It is timeless because it never loses its vitality; it never dies. It is safe because it never confuses the message of deliverance from all ungodly characteristics. It speaks without fear or favor. It is universal because there is no language in which it cannot be shared. It takes no account of race, color or condition in life. It is convenient because it can be easily understood and passed on to others who want to walk in God's purpose for their life.

God has so mercifully and graciously seen me through the experiences shared in this book and given me a heart to assist others to walk in spiritual victory.

I Truly Love You.

May God Bless You,

 In Jesus Name

## PREFACE

It is with unfeign, (genuine) faith, I believe many people in their homes, churches, communities and all over the world are living beneath the privilege God has purposed for their life. It is because of the false preachers, teachers and prophets running rampant in the Body of Christ in these latter days.

Jesus tells us that many are called, but few chosen.

Many people are chosen by men to come in the ministry because of their charisma, favor, money, long-time friends or relatives, more than not, are of themselves, not of God. People are not understanding, they are called to holiness and chosen by God after the trails and testing, in obedience in Spirit and Truth. Being not ashamed of the Gospel, allowing the light of Jesus Christ to shine in and through your life before all men. Then man chose you, because they see God shining in and through you in holiness.

You are chosen because you are God's desire. He chooses whomever He sees fit to do the work of the Gospel in spirit and in truth, without succumbing to the pressure of heretical ministers or other persons in leadership or positions of influence with methods contrary to God's Words.

### 2 Peter 2:1-3, speaks expressly of these people.

"But there were false prophets also, among the people, even as there shall be false teachers among you, who privily shall bring in damnable heresies, even denying the Lord that bought them, and bring upon themselves swift destruction. And many shall follow their pernicious (hurtful) ways; by reason of whom the way of truth shall be evil spoken. And through covetousness shall they with feigned (fabricated) words make merchandise of you: whose judgement now of a long time lingerth not, and their damnation slumberth not."

### 2 Timothy 3:1-7 speaks about the people in the latter days.

"This I know also, that in the last days perilous times shall come. For men shall be lovers of their own selves, covetous, boasters, proud, blasphemers, disobedient to parents, unthankful, unholy. Without natural affection, trucebreakers, false accusers, incontinent, fierce, despisers of those that are good. Traitors, heady high-minded lovers of pleasures more than lovers of God; having a form of Godliness, but denying the power thereof: from such turn away. For of this sort are they, which creep into houses and lead captive silly women laden with sins, lead away with divers lusts; ever learning and never able to come to the knowledge of the truth."

It's very important to discern them because you will see these people rise up from their respective places and begin to falsely preach, teach and prophecy to the Body of Christ. They have a form of God, but deny His power.

The sole purpose God has inspired this book is to bring his children in Love to one Heart, in one mind, one Hope, one Faith, one Baptism, one God, who is over all. Then you can honestly examine your heart to see where you are in your spiritual walk.

This book are experiences by application of the Word of God. Please read, meditate to be given the ability and power in spirit and truth to submit to change in every area of your life that does not represent Kingdom Living in the present world.

**Are you Standing in God's Principles, In Spirit and Truth? If so, the principles shall be your cover, because you have given the Word of God Authority over your life.**

Jesus says in Matthew 15 chapter, people make the commandments of God of none effect by their traditions and draw nigh unto Jesus with their mouth, and honor him with their lips for men to see; but their heart is far from Him.

In vain, they do worship Jesus, teaching for doctrines the commandments of men. Hear and understand it is not that which goes into the mouth that defiles a man; but that which comes out of the mouth that defiles a man.

## INTRODUCTION

We are now in the perilous times that Timothy spoke about and the evil spirit has come and is here now to kill, steal and destroy the Christ that dwells within you.

Your job is to establish a solid foundation in the Word of God, because without a solid foundation, built, equip, fortified and undergirded according to the Word of God, you shall follow the lust of the flesh, the lust of the eye and the pride of life. The lust takes you out of the will of God for the life God purposed for you in this earth, and places you in a backslidden state of mind.

The fruit of your ways will be the consequences you experience in this life. You must possess the Fruits of the Spirit (Love, Joy, Peace, Longsuffering, Gentleness, faith, Meekness, Temperance) those are the characteristics of God, the personality of Jesus and the actions of the Holy Spirit. They are all critical and vital possession in these latter days.

The problems people create, operating without the counsel of the Lord, will destroy their character, credibility, and true purpose in this life. Do not ignore God's Word as advice, even if it is painful for the present, it will keep you from greater pain in the future. The Word of God is firm in Love, it is right in Christ Jesus, and we are the righteousness of God.

The enemy wants to come in at the entrance of your mind and get into your heart to steal your joy in the Word of God. Peace, Love, Joy, and Hope is the rest while walking in the Word of God.

The enemy knows the joy of the Lord is your strength unto salvation. If he can destroy the faith you have in God's Holy Word (which gives you peace, love joy and hope) he can bring doubt and an unsettling in your spirit man concerning your salvation and direction and begin to lead you on a path that will destroy soul and body.

Let us keep in mind, satan spirit works inside out, this is why, satan spirit conforms us to put on a face as though everything is alright, while we slowly are deteriorating on the inside, then begin to leak or spill outward.

Remember that Satan will use things or people to place you in a situation that will steal, kill, and destroy your joy in the Lord. This keeps you from moving forward in your spiritual walk in Christ Jesus day by day.

God, who is rich in mercy and gracious, all knowing, seeing and everywhere at the same time, will watch over you while in the test of your faith, to create you perfect in every good work, to do his perfect will. A work well pleasing in His sight through Jesus Christ; to God be the Glory.

Let your conversation be without covetousness, strife, envy, unforgiveness; and be content with such things as ye have: for He hath said, I will never leave thee, nor forsake thee.

### Do not despise small beginnings

Philippians 4:6 reads, "Be careful for nothing, but in everything by prayer and supplication with thanksgiving, let your request be made known unto God."

**KEY:** Trust and never doubt. Do not lean on your
own understanding, but in all your ways
acknowledge the Word of God and the
Spirit of God will direct your paths. The pathway
is peace that passes all your understanding.
I am the Lord thy God, who teach you to profit,
And lead you in the way you shall go.

God is the Authority. Jesus is the Word manifested in the flesh. He is the water in that low, dry dead place in your life. The Holy Ghost is the Spirit of Truth that guides you on a path of righteousness, if you have Faith and trust.

Once you get revelation from God's Words, you will discern to the degree that allow you to be on a level where the Spirit of God can operate in and through your life fluently. It will give you the ability, power and authority to release God's Spirit over every evil spirit that comes to try you.

Yield to the Holy Spirit, the Holy Spirit will create in you a clean heart, and renew a righteous spirit within you.

You will have the mind in you, which is also, in Christ Jesus. Jesus, who being in the form of God, thought it not robbery to be equal with God, but made himself of no reputation, and took upon him the form of a servant, and was made in the likeness of men and being fashioned as a man, humbled himself, and became obedient unto death, even to the cross.

You must do likewise, so that our Father in Heaven will feel your heart yielding to his Holy Word. You will be transformed by a renewed mind. Jesus will bring peace, joy and love to the very being of your soul. "Our Father which Art in Heaven" will be looking at the Word made flesh in the earth.

The Father delights in such that seek after him. Our Father in Heaven is looking for himself in his children. He will be well pleased and act on your behalf, if you faint not. Because, without Faith, it is impossible to please God.

Keep your heart alive with the prayer of faith and works, because faith without works is dead and works without faith is not built on eternal foundation.

Now allow me to share my life experiences accompanied by the Word of God that taught me how to Build, Equip, Fortify in Faith to Walk in Spiritual Victory.

**BE A DOER, NOT A HEARER ONLY!**
**ARE YOU LISTENING?**

**KEY: BY FAITH, ABRAHAM WAS COUNTED AS RIGHTEOUS**

**THE JUST SHALL LIVE BY FAITH**

# CHAPTER 1

## ENTER IN TO RECEIVE WISDOM

## WISDOM TESTIMONY

Wisdom's starting point is God's Word revealed.

"Wisdom is the principal thing; therefore get wisdom: and with all thy getting, get understanding. Exalt her and she will promote thee: she shall bring thee honor, when thou do embrace her. Wisdom shall give to thine head an ornament of grace: a crown of glory shall she deliver to thee. "

The scriptures say to forsake her (wisdom) **not** and she shall preserve thee: love her (wisdom) and she shall keep thee.

Operating according to God's Word without revelation or following carnal truth are dangerous, it's relying on thoughts out of your free will. Spiritual truth from the heart are beliefs revealed by illumination (to give light to, to make plain) from the Word of God for your life.

Wisdom is the ability to make sound choices and decisions based upon the Word of God.

Wisdom is the ability to rightly divide and understand the Word of God in Spirit and Truth.

Wisdom gives you the ability to know it's not about the church, organization or building. It is about being in the Spirit of who God created you to be, and the move of God, to be a blessing and a living testimony, that brings hope to man-kind in this present world.

Churches (the church is you) are falling away because there are very few doers of the Word of God in spirit and truth. People are seeing too much move of man and not a move of God, so the Word becomes of no effect to the hearers.

Wisdom gives you the ability to know it is all about living the life of Jesus Christ in spirit and truth. No matter what is before you.

Finding true seekers in the Word of God is like looking for a needle in a haystack. They are not easy to find, they are set apart to do a perfect work in Christ Jesus.

The saints of God are filled with peace, hope, joy, wisdom, in the Spirit of Jesus with His love in their heart and fully persuaded we cannot do without his Holy Word in this present world.

God's wisdom gives the ability to hear with clear reception. Clear reception is studying to show thyself approved a workman that can rightly divide the word of truth. Not waverly in the path you professed the Holy Spirit has directed you to and in.

However, if you should leave the Word of God and govern your life by words contrary to the God's Word, you will be tossed around in the earth, subject to every wind and doctrine. You will be like the radio that loses clear reception, because the signals are no longer pointing in the direction of how it was originally built and programmed by its maker. Now if you should want the radio back to the original state, you will need to return it to the maker to receive true satisfaction. God is our original maker. God created male and female, he created thee. Do not be wise in your own eyes, turn to the one who knows the intent of your heart and only then will your land be healed.

Draw nigh to the Word of God, be a doer and your reception (i.e., ability) to receive clear instructions and get direct directions from the Holy Spirit will be satisfaction guarantee, if you **Do Not Lose Heart**.

### Wisdom are bookends for life

### Wisdom comes in two ways:

1. **It is a God-given gift. A gift you do not deserve, "Grace."**

2. **It is the result of a person's energetic search within accompanied in unconditional love.**

Now wisdom gives to those who seek earnestly.

Jesus loves a seeker, he said to the woman at the well that he loves such a woman that seeks after him. Jesus waited at the well, for a women the whole town despised, and until she was ready for a drink of living water. Jesus did not offer her a drink. He just spoke loving prophetic words to her, which caused her to examine her lifestyle, and see even though we are different, this man spoke substances that has changed my life forever. After those words she said "Give me a drink," then she dropped her pots and ran to tell the whole town, "Come see a man inspite of our difference, he loved me enough and told me things about myself that nobody else knew and his Words has changed my life."

God's wisdom is hidden from the rebellious and foolish.

God's wisdom is too high for a fool. The pathway to wisdom is strenuous. It takes a great deal of effort, but it's profitable, which in return becomes effortless.

David said, "Early will I seek thee."

David's son, Solomon, said, "Give me now wisdom and knowledge that I go out and come in before these people."

Solomon knew that operating from God's wisdom and knowledge was what he needed to stand before the people.

Jesus said, "Ask and it shall be given unto you."

Wisdom takes you to a secret place to know how and what to ask in prayer for God to reward you openly.

Seek truth and you shall find the revealing path. Knock with fervent, Sincere Praying with Praise and by Faith of works, it shall be opened unto you.

Oh, taste and see that the Lord's way is good. It is sweeter than the honey in the honeycomb.

How do you taste the Word of God? Be a doer of the Word of God.

We gain wisdom through a constant process of growing in the Word of God. To walk to and in maturity is to eat the meat of the Word of God. Desire the sincere milk from the Word of God, that you may grow thereby: If so, you have tasted that the Lord is gracious.

Hebrews 5:13-14: "For everyone that is on milk is unskillful in the word of righteousness: for he is a babe. But strong meat belong to them that are full of age, even those who by reason of use have their senses exercised to discern both good and evil."

God is speaking to our heart, the meat-eater desired to do His will, which allowed their senses to be exercised and tested to the degree they were able to discern both good and evil and made the choice to walk in the goodness of the Word of God.

We must trust and honor Our Father which art in Heaven. We must realize that the Holy Spirit reveals God's wisdom to us. We must make a life-long series of right choices by the Word of God to avoid moral pitfalls.

When we make choices by our sinful nature, we must learn from the error through the Word of God, by applying the Word of God in place of that choice made by a sinful nature. Be solid in the recovery through the Word of God.

We must possess discernment, which is the ability to detect good from evil (i.e., the difference between God's truth and man's fables), detect motives in the people. This is accomplished with wisdom in Love by Faith in the Word of God.

**KEY:** Be true to yourself, even when it hurts, for
after the hurt that is only to the body and mind.
The truth of God's Words will give Love, Peace,
Joy inside, and out of that is a lifting above your
circumstances, because Jesus has now filled you
with enough love in the heart by faith, that covers
the hurt in the mind and body.

### "LOVE CONQUERS ALL" "LOVE COVER SINS"

Many of you may believe wisdom comes with age, but the truth is, it comes with experience doing the Word of God. You must walk in the Word of God by faith, to see the signs and wonders that follow. Jesus said, "These signs shall follow them that believe." Jesus demonstrated the Word of God by given sight to the blind, healing all manner of diseases, unstopping the deaf ears, lame ability to walk. It was nothing but faith in God's Word that is greater than all, that tranformed these peoples life, for them to have the ability to live in the newness of who they were created to be in life.

**KEY:** Do you truly believe in the Words of God?
**IF SO, THEN LIVE BY THEM**

The evil days, we live in, with the negative influences in the world, cause spiritual problems. It is critical that you take a moment daily, to read and meditate on the Word of God, until it becomes your life.

The Word of God is your spiritual food you need in this life. It directs you on a path of love and righteousness. If you should follow your own words you may receive, temporary glory (goodness) but it has no lasting effect in your life and has a sweet, bitter ending.

While walking in the light of Jesus Christ, you can not share the glory. It is the spirit of God that points us in a loving and righteous direction, we followed according to the Word of God, and now we see a better tomorrow.

You have done the Word of God in Spirit and Truth, you have tasted the goodness of God, and know for yourself, he is sweeter than the honey in the honeycomb. You have establish a relationship with the Lord and Savior with a desire to never turn back to the world standards, because you know without a shadow of a doubt, He loves me. I was obedient to the Word of God in spirit and truth, it directed and seen me through life's obstacle, sent from the enemy to destroy me, but they were allowed by God to strengthen my Faith in the Word of God, and now I see better days that bring brighter tomorrows.

**KEY:** Do not allow these evils days to give you anything that will stop your forward motion in the Word of God. The children of God have been sent as light into dark places to be the answer people are searching for in these perilous times.

Nullify the desire of your flesh that would like to participate in the filth in this world. Remember, we are in the world, but not of this world. We are representing Jesus Christ and he came to seek and save the lost.

Wisdom is essential in your new Christian life. If any man lack wisdom, let him ask of God, that gives to all men liberally, and upbraideth not; and it shall be given him. Nevertheless, let him ask in faith, nothing wavering. He that wavers is like a wave in the sea that is driven by the wind and tossed to and from in the earth.

I have learned through life's experiences that living the Word of God is a wise choice. Always revert to God's Word in all matters or situations concerning your life and for others around you that may seek you for spiritual counsel. I know the out come is Victorious in Christ Jesus, if you hold fast to the Word of God and **Do Not Lose Heart**.

Wisdom taught me to think with my heart, not from trigger thoughts that shot in my mind. I learned the heart hears only good and righteous sounds. You must understand the heart is created to love only, however when it does not do what it has been created to do, it will become sick. Now the body will function from the trigger thoughts of the mind of your free will. But understand you are operating in a lower state of being, not truly who you were created to be and do in the earth.

Do not allow anyone to think for you, but respect, listen, and allow people to have their opinions.

Wisdom taught me to know if their values are not the same as those that govern my life. Do not give in to anything being presented or spoken contrary to your beliefs. Draw on the Word of God to overcome in this present world.

Wisdom taught me to stay in a positive frame of mind and not to speak those quick trigger thoughts that shot into my mind.

Wisdom taught me many times God allows misunderstandings to come your way, but it gives you an opportunity to bring understanding in that situation, in love, through Christ Jesus.

Wisdom taught me that I am not obligated to do anything outside of my value system.

Wisdom taught me not to have a hidden agenda.

Wisdom taught me to love people where they are and allow people to know they are valued, even if you disagree with their value system.

**KEY:** Jesus said, "Love thy neighbor as thyself," not follow your neighbor.

Be the light in the dark places in their life. Be firm and consistent in Love what you do and say to them. Believe me, their change is not in your timing, but in God's timing.

Through the years I have truly experienced God by being obedient to his Word. My upbringing was based on the scripture, "Train up a child in the way he should go, and when he is old he shall not depart from it."

My mother and other family members held onto the Word of God concerning my life, I tried to dismiss the teachings from the Word of God, because I did not believe that was the way I should live my life.

I would like to say, my mother is a Loving, and Great Woman of God that is very wise and loving with the abilities God has given her through experiences that has occurred in her life.

## WISDOM WILL BE YOUR PRINCIPLE THING, TO UNDERSTAND LOVE AND FAITH

Let us begin with my life experiences in order to bring deliverance in your life, through wisdom in Love.

Before I proceed, I would like the readers to understand that deliverance is what once governed your life according to the world standard, is now remove and replaced with the standards and principles according to the Word of God. God has given us power to overcome any obstacle that comes to try our spirit. **"The Secret Place"** he shall hide you; he shall set you high upon a rock. And now your head shall be lifted up above your enemies all around you; therefore you will offer sacrifices of joy in his tabernacle; you will sing, yes, you will sing Praises to the Lord."

**KEY: "Who the Son set Free, is Free indeed"**

### Can you truly tell someone, the Word of God set me free?

My story begins: I was living a lifestyle according to the prince of this world. The Holy Spirit apprehended me, God quickened Phyllis, who was in trespasses and sins. Where in times past I walked according to the course of this world, according to the prince of power of this world, the spirit that works in the children of disobedience, among whom also we all had our conversation in times past, fulfilling our desires with the lusts of our flesh, lust of the eyes and pride of life. We were by nature the children of wrath, but God, who is rich in mercy for his great love wherewith he loved me, even when I was dead in my sins, he had quickened me together with Christ by grace.

I had a choice, to continue being clothed in the old man, that sends me in directions that would destroy my soul and body and send my spirit to an eternal death or be clothed in the righteousness of God, and go forward in the things of God, not looking back with a desire to be in the old man, but only looking back with gratitude and understanding, praising Him that he knew and saved me before the foundation of the world, and before I stepped into time.

In my lowest state of being of the mind, the Lord spoke to me in a dope house. It quickened my spirit, which touch my heart. I dropped to my knees and said, "Lord, help me. I need you. If no one else in this house needs you, I need and desire your ways.

Before I go any further, my readers must be made aware of anger within a person. It is deep rooted, hidden spirit, and it is a silent killer. When it doesn't want to be reveal at that moment it hides in a **FORM of LOVE.** Anger has no hope, no future; it lives for the moment. Anger can not see beauty in anyone or anything, only self-righteousness. Anger can not see beauty in this world or a world to come. Anger has no face or feelings; it only feels its own hurt in which they do not want to feel, so anger programs the person with thoughts to mask over the anger that is causing the hurts in their life, in which it sends them in a direction that kills, steal, or destroy all in its pathway.

Understand many times this destruction is not seen with the physical eye immediately, but with the spiritual eye you can see the end results of what someone is speaking or doing.

If you truly love God, he will reveal to you what is happening in your life and around you. The only way it will not be revealed to you, is if you are following the lust of the flesh, eye or pride of life, because you have placed a partition between you and the principles, standards and moral convictions by the Holy Spirit.

However, since the angry person has nothing in place to comfort or assist in dethroning this spirit that has taken authority in their life, they will make decision that will not be for the good of man kind.

The Lord allowed me to connect with people of this nature because I had to identify the anger I had within myself, that was causing me to go in a direction of no hope and no future. This path allowed me to see and understand anger within many people that are on a destructive course in this life, with an eternal death sentence in this life and the after life. I truly did not understand God had a good plan for my life and that he could and would heal me everywhere I hurt, inpsite of all my wrong doings and short coming, and bring me to a better place in this life and the after life.

Now let us continue with my life experience. The man I had in my life at that time was full of anger, the day I wanted out of his life, his anger drove him to point a rifle at me in a dope house, calling me all kinds of obscene names, saying if I left him, he would shoot me.

I had to revert to the prayers to believe and trust what my mom taught me, that God is all that he says he is, his Word is not too short, the Word of God can lift you up where ever you maybe in your life.

I said Lord, I do not have any place to go. Everyone in my family including relatives has shut their doors on me. I prayed sincerely from the heart, Lord help and please lead me to safety. I know I have stepped out of your will in the most deadly ways, but I am sorry. Please forgive me and give me a second chance in life. No matter what comes and goes in my life, I will do only what you have purposed for me to do.

I do not want this life anymore and this angry man truly does not understand.

The dope man's best friend intervened and said, Man do not do it. Let her go.

Jesus spoke to my heart, Keep walking and do not look back or have a desire to go back. I have a hold on the trigger.

The Spirit of God began to direct me out of this house to someone I barely knew. The comforter was in control. Jesus spoke to my heart and said, I have this person prepared to receive you.

I drove straight to this person's house without detouring. I was running for a new look on life and was not despising the small beginning. I knock on his door and with open arms he welcomed me in and allowed me to make myself at home. I was very thin, homeless, with no sense of direction for my life.

I went so low in my life it seemed as though all the Word of God was not present with me, except for what my mom said, "If you can not remember any scripture, I want you to know you can call on the Name of Jesus to help you, and he will be there for you." "Jesus will be your present help in your times of trouble."

I experienced Jesus working through the person he lead me too, to assist in bringing me back to life, because I had a desire and will to live the purpose God called me unto. Not being wise in my own eyes.

**KEY:**   In revealed truth, a person's heart must be circumcised for his spiritual eyes to be open to see he is living in a state of being that has a destination where the end results will not be in his favor.

I would like to be true to my readers, and inform you that I tried to live according to my own free will from age 17 to 27. By October of 1987, I had enough of my own free will. I made a decision to live in the manner God had destine my life to be, before the foundation of the world and before I stepped into time. This is the very first time in 10 years, I ask Jesus back in my life, but I did not come with my whole heart, except with one foot in the world and one in the Word of God. But when I cried out to the Lord, I cried with every being within me.

In other words, once on safe ground, I became half hearted towards the Word of God, half under the blood of Jesus that cleanses. I would only do the Word of God when it did not interfere with the few worldly matters that felt good to my flesh.

In March of 1988, I was divinely delivered in a dope house from a worldly lifestyle in many areas of my life.
The Holy Spirit began ordering my steps Building, Equipping, and Foritying by teaching me the Word of God. The Word of God restored me to a new way of life.

In my heart, I began to feel grounded and assured in the Word of God, which gave me the ability to walk in my new direction in spirit and truth being an overcomer.

You feel like a baby trying to walk, eventually you will have Faith that believes and trust, and feel secure and comfortable from the spirit, soul, then body. At last, you feel strength, love, and hope, joy that brings peace that passes all your understanding. It is called 'blessed and assured that Jesus is taking care of the matters concerning my life and adjusting me in order for me to have wisdom with clear understanding, with a clear perspective on life, according to the Word of God.

When this happens in your life, you are filled with unspeakable joy. It puts running in your feet, clapping in your hands and a song in your heart. Your eyes begin to open and see with spiritual eyes. You hear from a heart of what the Spirit of the Lord has to speak expressively, that leads you on the path of righteousness for His Name Sake.

People will not understand, but you must say and know in your heart, they were not there when the Lord saved me, and they do not know what the Lord has done in and through me. If they will only watch your lifestyle, they will see that you have a Kingdom Living view on life, and out of a pure heart. Be an example and blessing to the people in this present world. Your testimony will always be appropriate.

Sometimes you will weep, because of the way you have been hit in your heart. Weep for the night, for God will bring joy in the morning. God wants you to understand this: understanding is a Peace that fills your heart with Joy, because it takes you in a direction to know they do not understand, but I know, I must and will be the example and yeild to the Word of God, because my life maybe the only Word of God this person may read.

### "GOD DID NOT SAVE YOU FOR YOURSELF"

The Joy of the Lord is your Strength unto Salvation. Salvation is a saving Grace, a free gift from Our Father in Heaven who Loves inspite of our short comings in this life.

This Love, Peace and Joy from the Lord provides a good quality of life, that gives you the ability to live in this world on a high octave note that travels like light. Jesus tells us we are the light of the World, a city that is sits on an hill, that can not be hid. Since light travels faster than sound, and Jesus is the light of the world, then we know and trust His Words will travel faster than the sounds our word makes in this present world. Let Jesus light shine before men, and they will see your good works, by the lifestyle you live in the light. This is why it is critical and vital to live according to the Spirit of who you were created to be.

You must understand, God see our tears, knows our hurts and feels your pain. God knows our thoughts and the intent of our heart from afar off. The only way the morning shall come is to receive by Faith and Believe and trust the Word of God with an understanding, that God's word will heal a broken heart, mend wounds, set captives free, giving liberty, sight to the blind, undo heavy burdens, teaching me to profit, leading me in a way I should go, and restore years that was stolen. Understanding, all things do work together for the good for those who love the Lord, and have been called according to His purpose. Your adversary knows this and will come to try you. If Jesus Faith was tested, so our Faith is tested. So, count it at all Joy.

**KEY: This walk in Christ Jesus gets better, if you can stand and stay the course.**

I would like my readers to know I searched for satisfaction everywhere I could think, in order to prove my way of life was right. But in this process, I discovered life without God's wisdom is a long fruitless search for enjoyment, fulfillment, and meaning in life that leaves you dead on the inside, and because the search came from evil, selfish, perverted motives and deeds, the end was sorrowful and fruitless.

I found that true happiness is not in my power to accumulate or attain wealth and material goods, because circumstances are beyond my control, anything that is not founded and built on the Word of God will be snatched away.

Today, people are still searching. They are not truly realizing they are fulfilling the lust of the flesh and eyes and pride of life. They want others to think they have the same control as God. By this, they are caught in the pride of life, which are just their opinions. They have an ownership mindset from a reglious or political view that mask their heart with pride and does not allow them to see the love in what is being done, because of possession and position, but you must understand that God made stewards, which places you in a different mindset, with a love in your heart for the good of all man-kind.

God is the owner of everything. God created good and

Faithful stewards. We are to manage what God owns with the abilities he has given in love out of a pure heart, governed by the Word of God, for the good of all mankind.

Peter said, in the third chapter of Acts that when the lame man was healed at the gate of the temple, which was called Beautiful, that all the people ran together towards Peter and John in the porch that is called, Solomon's, greatly wondering. Peter saw it and answered unto the people, You men of Israel, why marvel at this? On the other hand, why look so, earnestly on us, as though by our own power or holiness we had made this man to walk. The God of Abraham, Isaac, and Jacob, the God of our fathers, has glorified His son, Jesus. He was brought before Pilate who was determined to let Him go. They denied the Holy One and the Just, and desired a murderer to be set free unto them; and killed the Prince of Life. God hath raised Him from the dead; whereof we are witness, in his name through faith has made us strong, who you see and know: yes the faith which is by Him has given him this perfect soundness in the presence of you all.

I want to enlighten you that the same ownership spirit that chose Jesus to be killed instead of the true killer, is the same organizational spirit working in the earth today. It is in the work place, in the school systems, in the military, in your homes, in organizations, in government and unfortunately, it is in the churches.

When you operate from the Spirit of God in your prosective place, more than not you will be voted out. Many people do not understand that God has placed them in position to be a good and faithful stewards with the power of Jesus Christ governing their life. However, many people will fall prey to the prince of this world that blinds men where they separate the Live and Active Word of God from the church, work, school, vacations, etc.

Children of the Most High God, come back to your first Love and Have Faith in God's Word. Those that would like to exercise their free will, that was given to them by God, pray for them and turn them over to God. He will handle the matter in his timing, and if not in this life, it will be in the after life, but as for you and your house serve the Lord.

**KEY: ASK FOR THE LOVE AND PATIENT TO DO THE WORK YOU HAVE BEEN COMMISSIONED TO DO.**

I must enlighten you that people will put you in positions to make you feel like the power only works in and through them. In your heart understand and see that you are with a man that is blind. God is no respect of a person. What he has done for and through one person, he will do for another, if they hold fast to the Word of God and faint not.

Never allow people to make you think you have it all.

Never stop learning and growing in the Word of God.

Keep seeking God's face by prayer, supplication, with thanksgiving and fasting, knowing in your heart that you can do all things through Christ who strengthens you.

**KEY:** Be a David, Go for the **HEART OF GOD**.

I also, realized in my search that the more I attained, the more I wanted, but I realized how empty I was on the inside. I began to get real with myself because nothing around me was built and girded with the Word of God. I found that no pleasure or true happiness is possible without God, and without God the search for satisfaction is lost.

King Solomon speaks to us in Ecclesiastes, "Vanity, vanity, all is vanity."

I learned and have faith to seek the Kingdom of God and it's righteousness and everything else will be added to me.

Above everything in your life you should strive to know, honor, and love God's Word that is and is to come in your life. It gives joy, love, peace, hope, knowledge, understanding, and wisdom liberally and without restrictions.

The Word of God gives you the ability to stand with peace of mind when everything around you is falling apart. This comes with having God in the equation, because confidence in your own efforts, knowledge, education, abilities and human wisdom has no lasting reward or benefit in your hard work. I know from experience that nothing in this world can satisfy the deep longings in your restless spirit except God's Word.

Human wisdom or knowledge does not have all the answers, they are limited because it comes out of the world's education that sits in the seat of the mind, which

we know God had to break Jesus to the point of his skull, where He had to let go of thoughts from his mind and revert to the Heart of God and say:
**"Father not my Will, but thine Will be Done."**

To understand life, we need God's wisdom that can only be found with a heart that is thirsting and listening to the heart beat of Jesus, by seeking first the Kingdom of God and all His righteousness.

Listening to God's wisdom will spare you from the bitterness of human experiences. It gives hope that goes beyond this life.

I have found through my life experiences, that God judges, even the idle words, because they are in the heart. God is constantly dealing with the issues of the heart of man, which is the true you. Seek to possess clean hands and pure hearts, it will keep you from many hurts in this life.

**KEY: BEATITUDE: "Blessed are the Pure in Heart, for they shall see God."**

Learn to speak and live wisely, knowing that Jesus is interceding on your behalf, Our Father is watching and listening. You do not know the day or hour in which he will return for your soul, so live everyday as though His return for your breath of life is today.

I found that God gave me wisdom and understanding with the ability and opportunity to use time wisely and effectively.

I would like the readers to know and understand God has a plan for human destiny that goes beyond life and death in this present world, as we know it. Jesus said, "Fear not them which kill the body, but is not able to kill the soul, but rather fear him which is able to destroy both soul and body in Hell."

**"DO YOU BELIEVE THERE IS AN ETERNAL DEATH?"**

Let us think about when Stephen was stoned to death or when John the Baptist's was beheaded. Let us not forget Jesus, the torment he suffered in his body, boring our sins. All these great men knew how to hold on to the Spirit of God whom they represented in their present world in which they lived. They understood that the body would return to the dirt of the ground, the soul holding the spirit containing the Word of God would return to its original place with the Father which Art in Heaven.

**KEY**: Believe with a heart that trust the
Word of God to the degree that you walk
By Faith, not by sight.

## SATAN KNOW THE WORD OF GOD AND BELIEVE IT!

Let us look at the two robbers that were on each side of Jesus while he hung on the cross on Golgotha hill. One knew he had sinned greatly, and knew Jesus was an innocent man and was the Son of God, so he asked forgiveness. Jesus said, I will see you in heaven. While the other robber thought, if Jesus could not get himself down from the cross in the physical, how can he save me, so chose not to be forgiven of his sins.

Many people are like the theft on the one side of the cross of Jesus, if you can not stand before them at that time and perform what they ask so they can see, they truly do not believe and will say there is no God and no life after death.

There are people in this world who is like doubting Thomas, they must see and touch before they trust what you are saying.

Those stories were left for our learning, because God knew in this world many people are of the theft that felt, if I can not see your power now, I will not believe to do what is spoken from the Word of God.

## KEY: LET US NOT FORGET LIGHT TRAVELS FASTER SOUND. SEND THE WORD OF GOD OUT, IT WILL NOT RETURN VOID.

Pray, "Our Father in Heaven" Spirit will come alive in your heart and direct your soul, so the body will be in line with the very being of who God created you to be, before the foundation of the world, and before you stepped into time.

When we stepped in time, we lose conscience of who God created us to be in this world, because we where born in sin and shaped in iniquity. In other words, God knew where he sent us was a sinful place and he understood, if we did not gain conscience of him, and get back in fellowship with the relationship we have with him, then we would do the sin we were born into and shape to do.

I found, in my search, if we just seek the things of God, in which has been purposed for our life, it will free you from scrambling for power, approval, money, or popularity.

The fear of God is the beginning of knowledge. So, fear and honor God throughout your life and fill your life with serving others. It will bring unspeakable joy.

Your search for wealth, pleasure and success will ultimately lead to disappointment. Work done with the wrong attitude and motive will leave you empty. Work accepted as an assignment, is a gift from God. God's gifts bring joy to the heart and give you the ability to go in the direction of God's Word in spirit and truth.

In my wisdom experience, I have learned to apply and govern my life according to God's Word.

It is important to be a doer of God's Holy Word. It truly enhances your lifestyle, set a tone in a high octave in your life that brings peace, hope, love, and joy.

Let me remind you of a worldly phrase that is commonly spoken, "If we do the Word of God, you will miss out on the fun in life."

**DISMISS IT FROM THE HEART – IT IS A SET UP FROM THE ENEMY.**

When you trust the Word of God for your life, fun will become unspeakable joy that brings love and peace to your life. Fun does not and will not bring peace, because fun is from your free will, which you created without the Word of God, so you are subject to operate from a perspective of "anything goes." Joy comes from the Spirit of God that gives something greater than the world can give or offer, it allows you to enjoy life in a respectful manner.

Oh Taste God's Joy and see the Word of God is sweeter than the honey in the honeycomb. Allow the Holy Spirit to lead you on the path of righteousness for Jesus' Name Sake. The outcome will be Glorious and Victorious.

As I said earlier in the book, many things you do and say according to the Word of God will feel uncomfortable and not look right to you, because you are accustom to your free will. What you perceive as right from the world's perspective. It will be uncomfortable doing the will of God, because you are not accustomed to operating from the inside out. You have governed your life from the outside to make the inside feel good, and this way is not how God orchestra's your life.

Let go of those familiar spirits and old ways of life. Trust the Word of God with your whole heart. Never doubt. Do not lean on your own understanding, but in all your ways acknowledge the Word of God and the Holy Spirit will direct your path. The Holy Spirit way is peace, which passes all understanding. Yield to God's Word to be transformed by the renewing of your mind.

**KEY: BEHOLD ALL THINGS BECOME NEW**

The righteousness of God will see you through your darkest hour. So, walk by faith, not by sight. "Without Faith it is impossible to Please God."

Hebrews, chapter 11, speaks on the hero's in Bible time that walked by faith. By faith Noah, being warned of God concerning things not yet seen, moved with fear, and prepared an ark to the saving of his house. By faith Abraham when he was called to go out into a place that he should after receive for an inheritance obeyed. Through faith, Sara received strength to conceive and delivered a child when she was past age.

We must exercise our faith by believing and trusting to receive the will of God in and for our life. Keep in mind satan know the Word of God and believes, but his ultimate goal is to stop you from trusting. Trust is the key to be a Peter and step out of the boat by the Word of God.

To my readers I would like to end my wisdom testimony with ministering this to you: For those of you that are living from the world's perspective, or if your loved ones are living a life from the world's perspective, just remember that God has given all free will. But believe and trust in your heart that their free will is not God's will for their eternal life and no one can change them except your prayers to "Our Father in Heaven", who is greater than all.

I have faith to believe and trust, the same God that changed my life, can change yours and your loved ones' too. Pray, asking God's Mercy and Grace upon their life and He will give them a spirit to call out and pray for themselves, out of a sincere heart, to do the will of God with their whole heart in spirit and truth, for then they will be change, because they heeded to the Call, then they will be Challenged to see if change is rooted in their spirit and once you pass the test and make it through the trials in life holding on the the Word of God, you will be Chosen by God, then Commissioned to go out and tell somebody about how the Word of God saved you from danger and change your life for the good.

> **KEY:** Pray without ceasing, because Prayer changes
> things. Prayer makes a difference.

Understand my mother, sisters, cousins, saints and friends tried to tell me I was on the wrong path.
They spoke the Word of God to me, but the more they told me the righteousness of God, the more I rebelled against the Word of God and slipped further into darkness.

I looked at what people were doing in their human ability, and did not truly understand they were not conscious of their free will verses God's will for their life. Since I was blind, I had to go through experiences that allowed the scales to fall from my eyes to see the righteousness of God, verses what I perceived as righteous from the teaching of man's will.

The experiences have truly enriched my life to a level, to just have faith-that-believes and trusts in the Word of God with my whole heart, for my life and others the Lord send or I go down their path to minister too in prayer.

**Take note:** that a rebellious person does not hear and understand the things of God and can not see how it is beneficial for their lifestyle. They are so, comfortable with their life they can not see their way of life as dangerous or unhealthy. They can only be reached through your prayers and your lifestyle. Be an example in the Word, deed, conversation, conduct, love, spirit, honesty, faith, and most of all in holiness. All these attribute shows them good, clean living that can be trusted. Even if true Christians go wrong or fall short of the Glory of God, your heart will convict you to be honest in that fall, and turn from that wicked way and go in the direction of the Word of God in spirit and truth.

Satan spirit has no power over God's will, and can not force you to disobey God's Word. His strategy is to gain control over your free will by tricking, deceiving or tempting you into yielding your free will to his through fleshly desires, which is disobedient to God's will.

Keep in mind fleshly desires always hurt all involved by its actions, because it only thinks of self-gratification. You will be held accountable for your actions, if not in this life, it will be in the after life.

> **KEY:** Are you a willing vessel for the Spirit of God to work in and through, to do a good work by serving others?

God's Word never fails. He said, "Upon this rock, I build my church and the gates of Hell shall not prevail." Upon revealed truth, God will build his church and the passage way to eternal death will not succeed.

I am a witness. He will not fail you, if you build, equip, fortify your lifestyle on God's Holy Word. Therefore, draw close to God and He will draw close to you.

In this Spiritual Walk, it may seem the enemy is correct in the beginning because he wants you to draw back from the Word of God. Remember, God said, "If any man draw back from his Word, he is not worthy of the Kingdom of Heaven.

God is Spirit, he needs a vessel to operate in and through to produce Kingdom living in this world.

**In Exodus 3:14, God said to Moses, "I Am that I Am." I know that God purposes and promises will always become reality in your life if you faint not. Let us move in the spirit in order to see "I AM."**

**"I" is a singular noun, meaning God will work alone, all by Himself. In addition, God added "AM." It is present tense and means, "will be."**

**When God opened my blind eyes to see "I AM" I see and have seen him working all by himself in the world today, it is truly amazing.**

**God demonstrated to Moses by commanding him to go to Pharaoh, tell him "let the people go" are "I AM" will turn the Nile River into blood. Pharaoh thought he was greater than all, because on his payroll was soothsayers, magician, and political magistrates, but "I" who works all by himself, "AM" in the present tense said it will be, so the Nile River turned into blood. Just as God alone said it will be.**

**In other words, God is saying to His people, if you trust in my ways and stop adapting to man way because they show you things in this life, I will turn the circumstances to your favor, if you have faith that believes and trust in the Word of God.**

God has placed me in AWE and has proven to me to be the creator of all mankind, the one with unlimited ability in the earth.

You will go through trails in this life, because many people can not see you are trusting in the God that is within them, and when you do not see God within them, you can not come into agreement with them, so they think you are trying to be better than them, but hold on to the principles in the Word of God and understand I might have to be a Joseph in this life, before I receive the greater reward.

God caused the physical universe to come into existence and created a multitude of spirit-creatures to do a good work in the earth. God has intimate knowledge of his worshippers. We should know God and acquire intimate knowledge of his characterisitcs and qualities.

The apostle, Peter, says in Acts 2:21, "Everyone who calls on the name of God will be saved."

We are reminded, there are those who choose to operate from free will to do evil in the earth, to try to affect our good out of a selfish and jealous mind set.

Understand in your heart God's goodness and righteousness is in this earth. The adversary will make things appear as though they are not working together for the good with his twisted theories. Nevertheless, hold fast to the Word of God, understanding God works all things together for the good for those who love the Lord and are called according to his purpose.

> **KEY:** Are you allowing the Holy Spirit to create in you a pure heart with clean hands, where it cleans up your life style and gives you a desire to do a good work in the earth?

I would like to close this wisdom testimony with this:

Satan will place a smoke screen in front of our eyes for you to focus on what you hear, feel and see, taste. They are physically there, but by Faith with Love you can overcome the obstacles that are in your path.

Psalms 23:4,5 speak, "You will walk in the valley of a shadow of death, but fear no evil, his rod (the Word of God), his staff (Holy Spirit) will comfort you. He will prepare a table in the present of your enemy."

In Psalms 23: 4, David let us know, it is just a shadow of death. We know a shadow is only seen when there is light.  In other words, Jesus is the light of the world and if we are walking by Jesus commands, his light allows you to see, it is just a shadow in your life, so fear no evil, for I am with you, who expels darkness, but if you chose not the light to shine in and through your life, you will walk in the shadow that sends you in a direction of fearing evil, because you are a part of the evil and may be taken down depending on who is ready for you to fall.

Know people will set up a situation to cause you to fall when you are walking in righteousness, but fear no evil, because what they meant for evil, God will turn for your good and use them as stepping stones to take you to the next level in your life.

**"God said, I will make your enemy your footstool"**

The higher you go up in Jesus Christ, who is the light of the world, the more intense the heat will be. Anything that is not pure must be burned out of your soul, in order for you to see who God truly created you to be and understand Kingdom Living in the earth.

> **KEY:**  You are a Diamond; A Beautiful Butterfly; An
> Eagle that Soars High.

Malachi 3:3 says, "He shall sit as a refiner and purifier of silver: He shall purify the sons of Levi, and purge them as gold and silver, that they may offer unto the Lord an offering in righteousness."

If God said, He will sit as a refiner's fire. Then to sit means, rest the body weights. Refiners' fire is an intense heat that is greater than normal heat. The situation that has been created in your life, God has given the permission in order for you to come to an understanding as to what principles are governing that place in your life.

Since God is in a seated position, understand he will allow the situation to be there for a while, but understand in your heart, Jesus Loves You, He is gentle and a sweet smelling savior, he will not force you into a way of life where there is no understanding of who or what principles are governing that place of your life. If you surrender free will to God's will, to be placed in the refiner's fire, there should be no fear, because you drank water (Word of God), that will sustain you in your time of trouble (fire).

Let us stop: refiner's heat, which is able to remove all substances and materials from a product for it to have a pure shine; this is the same process God does in your life.

God allows a situation in your life that sends you in a direction to be tested. Since you are saying you drank the water (Word of God) to never thirst again. God allows you to go in the direction that will create a refiner's fire, for you to see and know what spirit you are possessing concerning your driving desire, because where your desire is, so is your will, and where your will is, so is the deeds you will do, and the deeds you do will be your destiny.

**KEY:** Jesus said to the woman at the well, to take a drink of His water and she will never thirst again.

The Holy Spirit leads us into all truth, so let us look at this spiritual matter from another perspective: God's Spirit works inside the heart and allows an intense situation to be created in your life, for you to see the intent of your heart. The Word of God that you profess is living and abiding in your soul, is the water (Word of God) you drank, since we are in a refiner's fire, we will need plenty of water (Word of God) by Faith, are there will be **NO** steam, and you will burn in the matters that was created in your life and the enemy knows it.

**KEY:** Fire makes water change its content to steam, a vapor suspended in the air.

The water (Word of God) will cause the refiners fire (intense matter) to change it's content to steam, a vapor suspended in the air. The vapor suspended in the air, is the Word of God.

The Spirit of Our Father in Heaven that breathe a breath of life in you to become a living soul. He wonderfully made you in his likeness and image, to go and do a good work in the earth. If you withstand the intense heat you will be sending the Word of God in a sweet smell back to Our Father in Heaven.

We must go through the proving and testing to be purge from impurities of this present world, to become purified as gold and silver for the perfect will of God to be done in and through our life, so you may offer unto the Lord an offering in righteousness.

You are cloth in God's righteousness. "Blessed are those who are persecuted for righteousness' sake; for theirs is the Kingdom of Heaven." As it is in Heaven, so it will be in the Earth.

> **KEY:** Do not use God's righteousness as a cloak of maliciousness, for many that choose too the end results are deadly.

The purging is hard, because sometime we do not want to let go of the familiarity. Understand you are walking by Faith, not by sight.

Let us meditate on Jacob, to receive wisdom with understanding in our closing in Wisdom.

Jacob came to a place in his life where he realized he was on a path of many dishonest deeds, but through a dream, understanding came to him, who God is and Jacob realized God Loved him, in spite of his short comings from his past life.

Jacob began to truly come to understand the God of Abraham, the God of Isaac his father, will be his God too. Jacob was wonderfully made; grace and mercy had been with him through all his dishonest deeds. He now had courage and hope in his heart to fulfill his purpose.

After some years, God told Jacob to go back to the land of Canaan. Understand after you are purged with a refiner's fire from unrighteousness, God will create a situation for you to go back to that place to bring closure with true love.

One night Jacob rested by a stream. Stream represents the continuous energy of the Word of God that is flowing in Jacob. While Jacob rest by a stream an angel had an effect on him, they wrestled so hard Jacob strained his thigh. The strain represent

Jacob was stretching beyond his proper limit, he put effort to assure he was doing what God had called him to do, because he desired God.

No matter how hard the angel tried, he could not overcome Jacob. This represents, Jacob holding on to God with all that was in him, no matter what the out come would be. Jacob said, **"I WILL NOT LET GO UNTIL YOU BLESS MY SOUL"**, because he understood the God of Abraham, Isaac and now his God had to bless him inside, for the outcome of the reunion to be peaceful, loving, joyful on his return to Canaan.

The angel asks Jacob what is your name, Jacob answered Jacob is my name. The angel says your name shall be no longer Jacob, but Israel, for you have wrestle with God and won the victory.

The angel from God, blessed Jacob in that place and Jacob called it Penuel, "The Face of God, for Jacob had met God face to face.

**KEY:** You must come to a place in your life as Jacob did to understand, before you can go back to bring restoration to broken relationships, dishonest dealing, ungodly character, you must hold on to the Word of God with all that is within you, by reaching beyond your human ability to something greater than yourself and ask for God to bring unspeaking joy in love to your soul to comfirm you are on the path he created for your life, then people from your past life will see the change inside out.

Always count it at all joy when you are in various levels of temptation. It's a test of your faith. So, be not weary in well doing, for in due season, you shall reap a harvest, if you faint not.

Many people get frustrated and say, "I cannot do it," but be an overcomer. Everyday you are living in this body in this earth you will need to overcome something. The world has a way that seem right unto man, but the ends is destruction.

You and I cannot do it without the great "I AM" living and abiding in our soul. Otherwise, we will be operating from a humanistic perspective, which rely on weak, imperfect, ineffective responses. Yes, this is frustrating. Wait upon the Lord for his responses!

As I once lived a worldly lifestyle, my mother would tell me she will not contribute to the lifestyle I was living. She would only pray and leave me in God's hands. I am very thankful that she held to those words, for I would
not have a relationship built, equipped, fortified in the Spirit of God, and know he is truly real and there is an adversary out there trying to destroy us.

**KEY:**  Concerning your loved ones, have faith-that-
  believes. Trusts the Word of God is like fire,
  a hammer that break rocks in pieces.

## Rock represents the hardness that has been formed around the heart.

Concerning your loved ones, have faith, believe and trust that God's Word is powerful, quick and sharper than a two-edged sword that divides the truth from falsehood, to know the intent of the heart.

Concerning your loved ones, have faith-that-believes and trusts that God knows what it will take to bring them on the path of righteousness, because He is omniscient (all knowing), omnipotent (all powerful) and omnipresent (everywhere at the sametime).

Keep in mind that we are speaking about a spirit that will need willing vessels to operate in and through in this earth. Just pray for the will of God concerning their direction and have a faith-that-believes and trusts that through your prayers, the love of Jesus Christ will see them through their darkest hour.

Your loved ones will need to experience Jesus for themselves, because they will meet him by themselves.

We all must work out our own soul salvation with fear and trembling.

Be there for your love ones, if they ask the counsel of God's wisdom for their life's situations, because we know the wisdom of God will keep them from walking in the way of ungodly counsel.

**KEY:**  I experienced the Holy Spirit as my teacher. I
  know Jesus for myself and, "for this cause I
  also, suffer things, nevertheless I am not
  ashamed: for I know who I have believe, and I

am fully persuaded that he is able to keep that
which I have committed unto him against that
day." 2 Timothy 1:12


"I am fully persuaded that neither death nor life, nor angels nor
principalities nor powers, nor things present nor things to come,
nor height nor depth, nor any other created thing, shall be able
to separate me from the love of God, which is in Christ Jesus our
Lord." Romans 8:38-39

CHAPTER 2

ENTER IN TO RECEIVE
FAITH & LOVE

## FAITH & LOVE TESTIMONY

If you are faithful to the call in love, that chose you and keep what God purposed for your life clearly in your heart, it will keep you from pride and sexual desires, which are the two most deadly sins in this world.

Let us talk briefly concerning two spirits I experienced that will keep you, as it did me, from Faith and Love in Jesus.

You have wisdom, but the wisdom is without the Love and Faith of God in your heart, so wisdom is to no good effect. You are being wise in your eyes only.

Now, when you are in the faith-love walk, beware of the spirit of pride and sexual immorality. Both are seductive spirits. Pride says, "I deserve it." Sexual desire says, "I need it." Their appeals are deadly to the spirit-man. If you are not walking in the spirit, you will fulfill the lust of the flesh. It is your body responding to the soul, which contains your emotions, thoughts and decision-making that has not been exercised in the Word of God. So, it is responding without the Spirit of God.

I know some will ask, "How does one walk in the spirit?" I will explain the Holy Spirit later in this book, but for now, the most important stand is to conduct and act only on the principles in the Word of God.

However, if you are not filled with the Spirit of God, which is His Word, you cannot see the attack on your life, until you are in this web of deception. By then, it can be hard to break free from those earthly spirits, and this is when you will need to reach deep in your inner beings for something that is greater than the stronghold that is possessing your life.

Pride appeals to an empty heart. A prideful, strong man does not want to see anyone do or be better than him. The roots of this spirit is self-centered and jealousy.

Let us take a spiritual look at Cain and Abel. Cain was self centered in his way of life and jealous that God accepted Abel's sacrifice and not his offering. Therefore, Cain slew Abel out of a prideful, possessive spirit, that contains self centered, jealousy, and self righteous.

Humans today operate from a Cain mindset. Instead of embracing the God given gift they have been given to operate in, in this present world and see how other gifts can be incorporated into their business, church and organizations, they try to kill your gift and promote their own opinions and ideas, they can not see team efforts, because pride looks only for self-achievements by the way of possession and position.

Allow the Spirit of God to open your eyes to pride, because the motivating factor behind pride is a conceited, possessive, selfish and jealous spirit, and through that spirit will come one or all these following attributes; revenge, competition, deceit, hatred, a lying tongue, no trust, anger.

Proverbs 16:18-20, Pride goes before destruction, and a haughty spirit before a fall. Better to be of a humble spirit with the lowly, than to divide the spoil with the proud. He who heeds the word wisely will find good. And whoever trust in the Lord **(Bless)** happy is he.

Pride will have you to speak in a manner as though you are better than anyone else, which turns to self-righteousness. Pride will not allow you to comprehend that humility is the way to succeed. A prideful spirit cannot and will not see humility at all as a way of life.

Psalms 73:6-9, Therefore pride serves as their necklace; Violence cover them like a garment. Their eyes bulge with abundance; They have more than heart could wish. They scoff and speak wickedly concerning oppression; They speak lofty. They set their mouth against the heavens, and their tongue walks through the earth.

> **KEY:** Proverb 13:10-11, By pride comes nothing but
> Strife, But with the well-advised is wisdom.
> Wealth gained by dishonesty will be diminished,
> But he who gathers by labor will increase.

Sexual desires appeal to an empty heart. The sexual desire of a strong man is whoredom.

I would like you to know that sexual desire is not just about the sex, but the love and desire of things for all the wrong reasons, and the act of sex, just happens to be one of the driving factors.

**KEY: Remember sex speaks on what it wants**

The motivating factor behind sexual is a spirit of whoredom and it's attached to love of the world, lust of the flesh, love of money and unbelieving friends that are not following the Word of God in spirit and truth.

This spirit will go after what it thinks it needs and people attached to the same spirit will go along with them as their support, because they feed on the need of what they are involved in in order to not to be alone.

**THIS SEXUAL SPIRIT HATES TO BE ALONE!!!**

You can only overcome these two spirits with a seek from within your belly, a hunger and thirst for righteousness along with a steadfast spirit in Christ Jesus, a commitment to holiness, and by the blood of the Lamb and the word of your last **TRUE** and **POWERFUL** testimony to come out Victorious in this present world.

> **KEY:** Jesus said, "We are overcomers, and those who worship Him, shall worship Him in spirit and in truth."

You should know that it was just the Word of God that you held in your heart as you walked it out in spirit and truth, and God Words seen you through your darkest hour.

God is no respecter of a person. What He does for one He will do for another in Christ Jesus, but you must ask out of a pure heart with the right motive, not out of self centered desires or greed.

**KEY: In Matthew 25:14-30, Jesus clearly allows us to see, the measure of talents were not the same, but truly wants you to use what was given to you to build greater.**

The servant with one talent did not understand, but Jesus knew his ability and did not give Him more than He could bare. The reason the man buried his one talent, he viewed it from a human perspective of what he felt he could do. He could not see how he could do anything with what he was given, not understanding the talent needs to be exercised through application of the Word of God to multiply to a greater protential, but he thought he was doing God a favor by burying the talent.

God wants us to see that it is not how much you have been given, but if you trust in the giver and have faith-that-believes, the giver will take you in a direction to develop and multiply your talent to be a blessing to you and to others.

If you possess an attitude like the man that was given the one talent by burying it, you will stop your talent from being developed and multiplying in the earth to be a blessing to the nation.

## KEY: Faith speaks what it believes and trusts in love

Faith and love are important qualities for your character in Christ Jesus. Both involve action as well as attitude:

- A faithful person believes the Word of God and works for justice for others through obedience to the Word of God.
- A loving person not only feels love in their heart for others, but acts loyally and responsible concerning the principles of love in the Word of God.
- Guard your heart with all diligence, because out of it flows the issues of life.
- Out of the abundance of the heart the mouth speaks.

Thoughts and words are not enough. God's principles must govern and guide our actions in this present world. We must examine our motives. Our lives must reveal we are truly loving and faithful to and in doing the work God has called us unto.

By prayer with thanksgiving and supplication let your request be made known to Jesus. Jesus said, He is a Wonderful Counselor. He will make the crooked way straight. The Comforter will guide you in the truth and what you pray in secret He will reward you openly. Let us wait on the Lord, so our strength can be renewed; that you may mount up with wings as eagles. You shall run in and through the Word of God and not be weary, walk in and through the Word of God and not faint.

**(Do Not Lose Heart)**

To receive God's counsel, we must be willing to listen and refuse to let pride stand in the way or sexual desires to interfere with us being a hearer and doer of God's Word.

> **KEY:** Pride says, his words and ways are higher than
> God's Words and Ways. Sexual desire says, I
> need something you can not give me.

Let us be obedient to God's Word, and understand we cannot be friendly with sin and expect our lives to be unaffected.

Love what God's Word is doing in and through your life. Hate the sin that is around you and in your life. Only desire to see a soul saved and set free from the wages of sin and death. Continue to be an example in spirit and truth, because God said, **"You are Your Brother's Keeper."**

Without faith, it is impossible to please God. God has given you faith-that-believes and trust.

You can do all things through Christ Jesus who strengthens you.

Love grows day by day. Love conquers all. Love covers all sin. In the battle, faith is a powerful weapon, and the power is activated out of humility in love. Jesus didn't want to go to the cross, He knew how much God loved us and what it would do for us, he said "Father, not my will, but thy will be done."

You can have the gift of prophecy, understand all mysteries, have all knowledge, and have all faith so that you can remove mountains, but if you have not charity (love), you are nothing.

### Read and meditate: 1 Corinthians 13:4-8

> **KEY:** Know that you can possess all the gifts of the
> spirit, but to God they are nothing, if you don't
> possess love. God will say, "Depart from me. You
> were a servant of iniquity. I never knew you." In
> other words, you did service for those deep
> hidden sins for man, it was not for the love of the
> brethren to see my glory (goodness) fill his life.

I have learned that faith and love is something you must possess in order to rest in the spirit of our Lord and Savior. We place faith and love in some people, (i.e., things we see), but we must possess faith and love in what we can't see, and come to a place where we feel in our hearts and know with understanding what gives us the ability to see the strength in who we believe and trust in.

We are more than conquerors, mighty through God to pulling down of strongholds, bringing into captivity anything that exalts itself over the Word of God, so we can discern who and what is trying to take resident in our soul to walk in the body we live in.

Now I would like to share my testimony of faith and love. The Lord had to place me in the wilderness on the backside of a desert, or so it seemed to me, because of the occupation in which I was employed. He took me out of computer operation and onto the road as an over the road truck driver, saying I must teach you faith and love.

I had to trust the Lord from the time I was in school learning how to drive, until the time I went on the road driving an eighteen-wheeler.

Jesus is my husband, friend and confidant. My close walk with Jesus has taught me, he will never leave or forsake me. As I walk in righteousness, he will hold my hand. He gave me a sign to know, He was in the equation. The Spirit of God spoke to my heart, "Phyllis, while on the road, no one will ever believe you are driving by yourself. They will always think someone is with you."

The other drivers did speak what the spirit had spoken to me, "Tell me that your husband is in the bunk, asleep."

Jesus gave me the inner ability to look beyond these truck drivers' outer appearance and trust in Him to protect me in all situations where the Spirit of God guided me.

I had to trust the Lord to keep me through the night, when I was driving in traffic or driving down dangerous hills where the starting point was high in the mountains with very bad weather. Ice that was so thick that it covered the highway for miles, if I made one wrong move, I would have rolled the truck on its side and slide down a steep embankment.

God will not reveal the whole plan to you. He knows if he reveal it, you will never trust him enough and walk the path he destine for your life. If he reveal the plan to you, surely you will not go down the path, you will think you took a wrong turn. He knows it is a struggle for you to walk by faith and trust the Word of God will take you to a victorious place in your life.

God chooses places that forces you to look at yourself in spirit and truth to be honest enough to say I need something greater than my or man's will.

I was in built in faith and love for God's will for my life and it gave me a greater relationship than my past experience.

I began to understand his love for others and me. I know he is always greater than the last experience in my life, because I have experienced it for myself.

I could sense Him speaking to my heart, giving me instructions and directions, though I did not see Him. I could feel and sense His warm caring spirit with spoken words that filled my heart with assurance, love and joy in the direction I was headed.

By having a wilderness experiences, Jesus showed me how his word operates to reveal. You must trust the Lord with all that is within you. You can believe, (satan believe) but if you do not trust, you will not move in the right direction and only from the move in the Word can you see the hands of God reveal his promises to you.

Deuteronomy 6:5 speaks, "And thou shall love the Lord thy God with all thine heart, and with all thy soul, with all thy might." We find the scripture saying to love God with everything that is within us. Since God is the Word, and we love the Word of God, then we will do everything in love according to the scripture.

Jesus came and reinterated the scripture, including the mind. In Mark 12:30, "And thou shall love the Lord thy God with all thy heart, and with all thy soul, and with thy entire mind, and with all thy strength: this is the first commandment."

Jesus came not to destroy the law, but fulfill it. Jesus knew through experience, the enemy's attack would be in the mind, which will build a shell around the heart. This is why HE said, be a doer in the Word of God out of a pure heart, and with clean hands, it keeps the mind clean. By being a doer you will see out of your heart are the issues of life, because what is in the heart is what you will speak.

There are many stories in the New Testament that clearly show us that many people were attacked in the mind. This is why we need to bring every thought into captivity and pull down strongholds that come against the knowledge of God's Word. If we desire the Word of God, we need to ask God, for He gives generously to those that call upon his name and wait for an answer.

Since the first commandment is too: "Love the Lord thy God with all thy heart, and with all thy soul, and with all thy mind, and with all thy strength," we know that if we do not exercise our spirit in the first commandment, then how can we follow any of the other commandments in spirit and truth, which our next command is to love our neighbors as ourself.

We can have all the gifts, but if we do not possess love (charity) we are nothing and we clearly are not serving the God of Heaven.

Now, let us look at the word (strength). It is what you trust in. Trust is a strong reliance on the integrity, honesty, and dependability of a person or thing. Trust can also be viewed as confidence or faith. If you have faith-that-believes in the Word of God, then trust and move in that direction for your life.

We must always operate from the Word of God are we will have a spiritual set back. It is like driving on ice or down steep grades from the top of a mountain. We must hear clear instructions and obey the directions on how to stay on the road. Some may say I was taught those principles in driving school. That is true, but just reading a book and seeing the movie is different than doing the actual application. In the same way, let us hear the Word of God and actually trust it enough to do it.

### KEY: DESIRE THE WORD OF GOD AND BE A DOER!

I felt Jesus speak to my heart to move me in safe paths. You must hear, have faith that believes and trust the instructions and direction that applies to your life from the Spirit of God. Understand in your heart, you are walking by faith, not by sight, and you will not see proof until you first obey by acting on what you heard, by Faith that believes and trust with your whole heart from the Word of God. Stay focused and receptive to God's Holy Word. A still small voice speaks to your heart, saying, **"This is the way,"** by God Words your heart will feel at peace in a resting posture, but if you are disobedient by not following in the path

God is calling you too, you will be in a restless state of being. Many times this state of being can cause fustration, confusion,

dissatisfaction. There is a war going on, on the inside good verses not so good, so the restless continues. Always no as in the story of Joshua and Caleb, the majority in many decisions is not the way to go, even though I know we live in a world that says the majority wins, but with God only through prayer will you know if the Hearts of those people are following the will of God for Kingdom Living in this earth.

Let us look at the story in Esther chapter 6, 7 to understand this restless state of being.

I knew God had a plan for my life. I just had to understand my purpose for being in the present world. By going through circumstances on the road my faith was building.

**KEY:** Keep in mind, God is building your faith and love, so tests and trials must come to try what is in your heart.

One day I was at home on a three-day break. God said, "Go look at the picture of the George Washington Bridge in your bedroom." As I gazed at the picture in a relaxed state of mind, He spoke in my spirit so plainly, "Your husband lives across this bridge."

I shook myself and came out of the state I was in, because my mind was not on a husband. Thirty days later I was in Dallas, TX., picking up a load at the company's yard, when I ran into my future husband, though not knowing that it was him.

To shorten the story, I needed the company car, but he was assigned to it to go to dinner. I was told if I needed the car I had to talk to the driver that has been assigned to it. I ask him for the car, but he said, "We can share the car and I will take you to dinner after you are done shopping."

We discuss many issues at dinner, eventually I asked, where do you live, he said, "Across the GW (George Washington) Bridge in New Jersey." I hardly spoke the remaining of the dinner. He said, you are quiet is something wrong, I said no. I was in amazement that he said the same thing that was spoken to me and I had never seen or known this man. We exchanged phone numbers and began to communicate through our dispatchers and three months later, we were married.

After we married, God began to work inside me to show me unconditional love. I truly did not know how to love anyone except myself. Jesus broke through the walls that guarded my heart by bringing two people in my life, my husband and daughter. Some might think you would know love through your mother and father, but it is natural to love your mother and father unconditionally because they only want the best for you and will not hurt you. I came to understand deep inside myself, even if you feel your parents hurt you, you can never feel a true hate for them.

True love is something you must experience within yourself before you can truly love anyone else unconditionally. I protected my heart to keep people away from me, but once Jesus opened my heart and ministered love to me, it was a new day.

The Spirit teaches, you can not guard yourself from people, because God has created all kinds of people with different customs and cultures and if they choose to operate out of their free will, we must respect, but not walk in their counsel, stand in their paths, or sit in their seat, but guard our Heart because we know and understand the prince of the air is in the earth roaming to and fro to seek whom he can devour.

God teaches that we must choose our friends wisely, not to be unequally yoked with someone that does not believe as you do. Delight yourself in the book of the law so it shall not depart from your mouth, meditate in it day and night, that you may observe to do according to all that is written there in it, For then you will make your way prosperous and then you will have good success.

**KEY:** When you are girded in the Word of God, pain becomes painless. You understand after the brokenness comes a blessing, if you are holding on the Word of God. He heals you everywhere you hurt.

Know that God sees the paths you need to take to bring deliverance in your life. I ask God "Why?" By asking, I learned why God wants us to ask "Why?" He wants to give us the true answer, but many times, we are not willing to accept what he is speaking to our heart. Often, we trust our fleshly desires, then say God said it, while the truth is, if we are grounded in the Word of God we can clearly discern the difference between human desires and God's desires.

God sees something in our life and knows you need to go down a particular path to bring true deliverance. You may have a form of godliness, yet deny the power thereof in a certain areas of your life. You may speak the Word of God with your mouth, but your heart is far from it. The path, which God allows you to take, will cut out whatever is not operating on God's principles, he has commanded us unto.

Do not resist the Word of God; allow the Word of God to flow in and through you to reach others, because true victory is only established with a solid foundation built on the Word of God.

God takes you in a direction that builds faith and love in the Word of God to be an overcomer while in this present world.

Believe me when I say, I would have never married my husband and brought our daughter into this world, if I had known my husband was deceitful, a cheat, verbally abusive and an angry man. Nevertheless, Jesus allowed me to go down this path, because I was once verbally abusive, deceitful, a cheat and angry woman. However, I had to see myself in my husband in order to hate what I was seeing and know that God had delivered me from the anger, cheating, and deceit and desire never to go back to that state of being. However, I still possessed a spirit of verbal abuse, and needed to be delivered.

**KEY**: However, one of the greatest lesson I learned, the Word of God is the water, satan cannot stay under the water (Word of God) to long are he will suffocate, therefore he sticks his head up for air, for you to see his true face. Moreover, it is always an ugly sight. This is another reason why patience is very important when operating in the things of God.

I have truly learned when you are living the life of Christ; God will convict your spirit, if you are going in a direction contrary to his will for your life. It feels as though God grabs you right in the heart to get your attention. In other words God brings you to a realization of your own guilt. Ask for forgiveness, In Jesus Name.

God **will not** continue to allow sweet and bitter words to flow out of the same fountain, if he is holding your hand. God knows

52

when you truly have a repentant and forgiven heart. Remember that you are being the fool when you pretend as though you are walking out the Word of God for your life. God knows all, sees all and is everywhere all at the same time and your sins will be found out.

**KEY:  GOD WANTS A RELATIONSHIP
WITH THE <u>TRUE YOU</u>.**

**WILL THE REAL YOU
PLEASE STAND UP AND COME FORTH!**

The enemy knows where you are in your walk in Jesus Christ. Satan will use whoever and whatever he can to get you off the path of righteousness. He used my husband to try to get me to stumble in my walk in Jesus.

Understand that God had a better plan for my life. Though I was in diverse temptations, it was testing
and proving time in the Word of God for my life; so, I counted it at all joy.

I had to love my cheating husband and his girlfriend in spite of their shortcomings. I had to understand and trust that God would have people come down their paths and plant seeds.  I understood I was one of their examples of Jesus Christ.

I had to keep in my heart that if a seed were planted in their life, God would give the increase that would cause them to grow.

Jesus taught me how to love in spite of what's going on around me. Jesus had to teach me to look beyond what was in front of me and see a much more beautiful place for me and the others involved in my life's situations. I did not want to reunite with my husband, because the more I told him to go right, the more he went left. I knew I had to pray in order to see him and myself in a better state of mind and condition of heart.

Jesus gave me wisdom and faith early in my Christian walk.  I had to learn Faith in Love according to the scriptures, without any conditions.

God was teaching me how to apply the wisdom-principles and faith-with-unconditional-love to see another level in the Word of God.

The goal of satan is to take the seed that is planted in your spirit, which is the Word of God, so you will **not** seek the things of God with that hunger and thirst for righteousness and revert to making decisions from your free will, which is your human ability. Man has knowledge and wisdom, but without the knowledge and wisdom from the Word of God.

**KEY:** What ground did your seed fall on?
By the wayside? On Stony Ground, Thorns?
or Thistles, or Good Ground?

My greatest test was this: I had been a housewife for almost seven years when my husband walked out on my daughter and me in order live with a friend, then eventually, his girlfriend.

Him and his girlfriend lived very close to our home. He did not provide living expenses for our home. His earnings were spent on his girlfriend, but the Lord gave me a vision that Jehovah Jireh would provide for my daughter and me.

My daughter was just starting kindergarten when God said to me to go to school with her and volunteer. I said, "Lord, I need income." God asked me to trust what he was saying to me. I asked, "Where should I go and volunteer?" He said to the library.

When I went to the school, I asked where is volunteers needed the most, they replied in the Nurse's office. When I asked if they needed any assistance in the library, I was told they could always use some help in that area.

When I went to the school the next day I went to the Nurse's office, but my spirit did not feel right assisting there, although the Nurse showed me how thankful she was in having me there to help.

The next day I went to school, I asked to assist in the library and they had someone escort me to the library. I felt assured, this is where God called me too. Later in the month I asked about a job and was told they had just hired someone.

I went home that night and cried, praying, "Lord, you told me to go there, and spoke in my spirit, to trust and do not doubt." You said you would supply my every need. I got up off my knees and fell in a peaceful sleep. I continued to go everyday as a faithful volunteer.

Since, my daughter was in an all-year-round school district. My daughter's nine weeks of school were over and we were going out for cycle break for three and one-half weeks.

Upon my daughters' return from cycle break, I faithfully went back to the library to volunteer. On my third day back the lady that was just hired before I started volunteer work, pulled me aside and asked if I was looking for a job, I said yes I am. She said, I put my two-week notice in the last week, this is my last week. If you are interested, you will need to inform the librarian.

This was God, I knew no one in St. Charles, MO., and we had only lived there three months, before my daughter started school. I also did not know, the librarian was a Christian and her husband was a minister in the faith, until I spoke to her concerning the open position.

To make a long story short, I filled out the application, was hired, and was able to work and be with my daughter while she was in school. This was a blessing for my daughter, and me because it kept us together, while I went through a reckless, divorce. God blessed me with a strong support system at church and school. Many teachers would say to me, "You are holding up great and your daughter does not seem as though she is affected by it at all." A lady came in the library to volunteer for three days, on third day she gave me a note and said this is from the Lord, it reads "Do not worry, look to your daughter, for she is your strength in this hour. Continue to go with the process.

Listen to that small peaceful voice and do not try to understand. He knows what is best for you and all parties involved, so do not allow that selfish spirit to get on you and think of yourself. Though your weary eyes cannot see, just say, "Thanks you, Lord," and do not complain. May God be Edified and Glorified in our life.

**KEY:**   God placed a song in my heart, I Am all you need to get by, even when the storms of life come or the wind blow, I am are all you need to get by. A song in your heart from God can carry you through the most terrible storms in life, it's like an anchor that holds you in the place you should be in.

My husband spoke in a very arrogant manner, sure of what he could do, and his girlfriend was in agreement with his way of life, which made the situation even more disgusting.

My husband would make people think he was giving me everything. He would pretend he did not want to hurt our daughter and I, but this was furthest from the truth.

**BUT WATCH OUT!!!**
**THE DEVIL WILL MAKE A FOOL OUT OF YOU!**

I am bringing my readers here to allow you to see, people must be honest with themselves as to why they are doing what they are doing.

Examine the motives as to why you are going in that direction:

- **Is it for self-gratification?**
- **Are you considering all parties involved?**
- **Are you making a decision on principles that will benefit all parties involved?**

If my husband was not doing anything to hurt us and wanted us to have everything and he just wanted to see his daughter. Why did he get a lawyer? If what he was saying was true. There only would be a need for one lawyer to write our divorce papers, then our signatures and it would have been over in thirty days, if we start from the seperation to the divorce it took two years and three months to be over.

The deceiver that works in the children of disobedience wants people to believe that my husband was giving us everything while it was actually the two lawyers fighting to make money from the both of us. But understand I didn't have any money to give. My lawyer and I had already made an agreement on a set cost, no matter how long it took and it was not even close to a thousand dollars.

Behind the scenes satan spirit had my husband to do a work for him that made a fool out of him. My husband went in a direction to try to destroy my Love and Faith in Jesus Christ, but he failed in the mission, and he destroyed his financial status, living condition, and job situation, and most of all his character of who he portrayed himself to be.

**KEY:** Understand a fool can't see himself working for someone that is trying to destroy his life and all others involved. If he could, he would stop before the destruction becomes unrepairable. Satan put the blinders on and sends a false sense of love and security in what they are doing, so a fool continues in his or her foolish ways, and only God can restore them.

Do not be a fool, for the lust of the flesh and pride of life. I found out for myself, before my marriage that satan spirit will cause you to go in a direction of your free will that will make a fool out of you. In that direction I lost a child and it was not unto death, I lost finances, creditablity, a place to live, a car, the characteristics of who I was created to be, but I had faith in God to restore to me the years that were stolen from me and he can do the same for you.

## "GOD IS NO RESPECT OF A PERSON"

At this point God desire was for me to remember He loved me while I was in my mess, so gird up with strength in the Word of God to assist in delivering my husband and his girlfriend from their free will that is controlled by their sinful nature, which is very destructive to them and   others. I had to Love with agape Love.

God revealed to me, no one will have an excuse as to why they continued to go in a direction that was not good for them and others.

I hope that while in the earth you pray a repentance prayer and ask for forgiveness in your heart, so on judgement day, Grace and Mercy will be standing to vindicate you.

Now, if someone does not care to repent, forgive, or be delivered because they choose their free will, God has given them a choice, but will also keep presenting an opportunity to repent and turn from their evil ways.

With Jesus on my side, I had to face two people that possessed a strong free-will spirit. Jesus knew, and equipped my spirit to be able to stand against the wiles of these free-will agents.

Over the next several months, I went through some things with my husband and his girlfriend that would cause some women to lose their minds. How many of my readers know that God is faithful to those who love Him, In Jesus Name.

Jesus kept telling me, "Hold on to my Holy Word. Take care of my child that is a blessing to you. It is going to get worse before it gets better because the enemy wants you dead in your spirit.

God spoke in my spirit, "Your husband was easy access for satan's spirit to use to try to lure you away from the faith and love of **"I AM"**.

Through the experiences, my husband has seen the end result. It was himself that suffered and hurt.

Men and women in the faith, whether it be both of you or one of you, never think for one moment that God will allow you to leave one covenant marriage and build a true relationship with another person, only in a covenant relationship can you receive the greatest blessings and fulfillment in this life and the after life. You will never receive God's Blessings and fulfillment outside of a covenant relationship or have true love and trust with another person without pursuing the relationship in a Christ like manner.

Many people do not understand relationships and God's principles that govern a relationship. So many people govern relationships from a physical stand point, this is why you will hear people make this statement "God knows we are only human." These people are free-will agents that govern their life based on their standards, morals, and principles, which cause them go and send others in a direction of outside in, **not** inside out.

I experienced my husband not being truthful to me and taking our daughter over his girlfriend's house, inspite of the principles and standards we were raising her under.

The girlfriend was not governing her life or her daughter's by any principles that are good for all man kind. She convinced my husband, his daughter was no better than hers and he need to bring her over to her house to be with them. You think I was going to accept this?

I will be honest with you, readers, I was not delivered in that place in my life. I still had fight in me, so God had to allow me to go down that path to see that I still need deliverance in that place of my life. I had to understand vengeance belongs to the Lord. He will repay. Be still and know he is God all by himself.

One day the spirit told me that my ex-husband was not being truthful in where he said he was going with our daughter. I gave him time to get to his destination, then I went to his girlfriend's house. There he was with our daughter. I pulled my car in the back of her house, threw the car in park, jump out and began to tell both of them, how low-life they were living in the present of children and her parents.

Then I rushed his girlfriend and started the fight. Her father and mother came out the door, saying help my daughter, my husband grab me, wrestled me to the ground, held me, and told his girlfriend to come get a kick in, he pick me up, and threw me in the car and told me to leave because he loved her and that is where he wanted to be.

Instead of praying to God concerning what was revealed to me, I step out of the Word of God and satan used me for his work.

God placed in my heart in a clear and peaceful way, **"Vengeance belongs to the Lord and I will repay."** Nevertheless, from that experience I did learn a valuable and beneficial lesson concerning the Lord's vengeance for a person's life.

    **KEY:**   I know this to be true, God can and will execute judgement in a person life greater than you or your free-will could ever do or think you can do.

I had to go through the same test one year later and I passed the test and obtained victory in that area of my life.

How do a person know you passed the test, is when you can see the other person in their earthen body, but see right through them to the degree that you see they can **not** do any better, because they do not know better. They will look foolish to you and nothing they do or say moves you. In fact, you feel sorry for the way they choose to speak and live and then you will begin to pray for their souls out of a sincere heart.

The Spirit of Truth speaks to the heart to inform you of the truth in all matters concerning your life or if necessary in others life. The revealed truth does not come to take matters in your own hands. It is revealed to us because we need to pray and have faith-that-believes and trusts in the Word of God concerning the matters we or others are facing in this present world.

Understand in your heart, God will take care of the circumstances in your life, even if He has to bring a strong wind into the circumstances to let them know it is His anointing they are trying to destroy, this He will do.

Believe me when I say, "God will bring a strong wind if need be."

Give people the opportunity to see themselves, know the desire for change is up to them. I understand people will never have true love, peace and joy in this life until they come to repentance and turn from their wicked ways, and only then will their land be healed.

God spoke to my heart, If you stand on the Word of God, pray without ceasing and leave them alone, I will repay, because vengeance belongs to me. It is not a flesh-and-blood fight, but a spiritual battle. I Am God, and the gates of Hell shall not prevail against holiness, if you hold fast to the Word of God and do not lose heart.

How did I hold on? I stayed in the Word of God, applying it to my daughter and my life situations, went to church, prayed, fasted, was still when Jesus put it in my spirit to be quiet and still, stayed around the mothers that were warriors in the faith. God blessed me with one friend to call, if I was saying anything negative, Jesus would have her to say to me, "Phyllis, what piece of the armor have you taken off? Put it back on and go to war." This was the best friend Jesus could have ever appointed to me during this time in my life, because she was a vessel from God to keep me focused on the things that were of God.

### I am thankful to Jesus for our friendship

I had to love my husband, in spite of what he said to me or what I saw. During this season of intense testing I understood and knew this was my proving and testing season.

Jesus told me to read the story about the Prodigal Son. This was very hard for me. I focused on the son and every time I got in prayer, Jesus said, "Read about the Prodigal Son." By the third time, Jesus said, "I want you to focus on the father, not the son, you must possess the father's character when associating with your husband and others that do not possess the Word of God in their life.

Your husband, his girlfriend and many others are out for the feel-good moment, which is a bodily experience, not an out of body experience. God spoke in my spirit, you once possessed the spirit of the Prodigal Son just as many people in the world do now, but through my grace and mercy you have been delivered and now have the mind of Christ Jesus. Some men and women choose to be blind, and their evil and perverted ways keeps them from desiring to live a respectful and worthy lifestyle.

God filled my heart with love and a song in order to make it through the trials in my life. I came to a place where he said, "No more a babe in the Word of God, for I have been pouring new wine into old wineskins, you continue to leak. Understand, sometimes a doctor must get his patient well and strong enough before he can do surgery. I must do the same with my people to possess the staying power in the Word of God, love all mankind no matter what the trial may be in life or in the life of the others you are appointed to assist in their spiritual walk,  for only then will you know you are a new creation, a Son of God.

> **KEY:**  God will continue to pour his Word in your
> heart until you are well and strong enough for
> him to cut the sin out of your Life with his two
> edged sword in Love. God will reveal to heal
> you every where you hurt.

I got in prayer and meditated on what He spoke to my heart. Jesus began to do surgery on my heart. I must say it hurt so bad I could feel the cutting in my heart. The pain caused me to fall to the floor in my kitchen in a fetal position and cry like a baby. I know God created a new heart, which renewed a righteous spirit in me.

It was hard to love in spite of what I seen and heard in my past. I felt a lifting inside me, as though the Spirit of the God stood me up from the floor, and God said, now you are a new creation old things have passed a way, behold all thing are new to you. I felt so much love it seem as though it was flowing out of my pores to the degree I smelled only sweetness. And from that day in July, 1998, all I know is that I love and pray for the brethren in spite of what I heard or seen, because they truly do not know what they are saying or doing in and to their life. They are blind men walking in the earth doing whatever their free-will says is right for them.

Some may think, people do know what they are doing when they come against the Word of God. Some people do know what they are doing from the world's standards of life, but their aims is to cause you to backup and not walk to strong or not at all in the Word of God. In other words, because they walk from a physical position they are blind and ears has been closed from a spiritual position, so they can not stop themselves from attacking your spiritual walk, so they continually travel a path that is leading to eternal death, and out of a Jezebel spirit they discern what they are doing, because their aim is to stop the Word of God from going forth and operating in this present world.

The strength in people heart to truly do what is good according to the Word of God has not been exercise to the degree or level where they can move from spirit to soul to body. So, it reverts to a physical position, i.e., what it can see, taste and feel, and from this perspective one can not truly see or understand the damage they are doing to themselves or others in this present world or even in the after life. Until the Spirit man inside is exercised, they will continually make decisions that pertain to the physical man of what they **feel** they want or need without consideration of others, and the Jezebel spirit can see and hear, but will not submit to God's Authority, that comes in HIS likness and image.

> **KEY:** In spite of my shortcomings I knew that Jesus Christ loved me and drew me to Himself. He will do the same for you, if only you have faith that believes and trust by application of HIS Words.

I know that love brings you into the presence of all man-kind, because to love Jesus you must love all man-kind. Jesus says, how can you say you love me who you do not see, and your brother you see everyday you hate. In other words, who you can not see you love, and He is spirit, and HIS Spirit may be abiding in your brother who you see everyday.

After I receiving a new heart. I saw a vision for me, my household, and I knew it was going to be a fight to attain it. But, "Victory was already mine," said the Lord.

Jesus demonstrated His Power to me in a mighty way by bringing my husband to a place in his life to seek the things of God. It was many times through prayer and soft-spoken words of God filled with love that he would hear what the spirit was speaking through me that he would apply them in his life.

This is the man that threw my bibles in the trashcan and said, the Bible was putting a wedge in our marriage and "Do not ever pick them up," are I will kill you. I said, well I will be dying tonight, because I am going to pick them up out of the trashcan right now. I went to get them out of the trashcan right in front of him, and this is the man that is seeking to know the Lord for himself.

The girlfriend admits her wrongs, but most of all, I hope and pray she asks the Lord for forgiveness and strength to never go down the path she chose again. I understand it is between her and God, so may God be Edified and Glorified in and through her life.

As Christians, if we stumble along the way, we must ask forgiveness quickly and turn from the evil way. We must continue to be a light in this dark world until we take our last breath or until Jesus returns in the Second Coming.

I cannot begin to explain everything that I went through in this book. My hope is that you grab hold of these true experiences. Trust and never doubt God's Word in all you do and say. Know that Jesus is always Love. Jesus' Love will see you through the darkest storm in your life. Be a Peter. Step out of the boat and walk on the water. No matter what you see in the natural or what your friends say contrary to the Word of God, keep your heart toward God's principles for your life. Pray to possess a steadfast faith, one that is unmovable and unshakable, and will always be abounding in the work of the Lord.

Know that faith without works is dead. Have faith-that-believes and trust what the spirit of the Lord speaks in your heart. Launch out into the deep and hold on to the anchor that holds who is Jesus Christ our Savior.

Understand when Peter walked on the water, the water represented the Word of God, God is our authority, the support in our heart. When Peter walked on the water; he was walking the talk. When his friends began to speak negatively, he took his eyes off the authority (the Word of God), his support, and he began to sink. Notice when Peter called for help and looked to his authority for assistance by reaching in Jesus' direction. Jesus was right there for Peter and will be right there for you.

In other words, Peter reverted to a human's physical view, regarding what he was seeing, hearing, feeling and tasting, touching which eventually caused him to fall in his spiritual walk.

In this world we know we can not walk on the water, but since the water represent the Word of God, Peter was walking by Word of God and people could not see his support, so they questioned his doings.

Recieve this in your heart, if you are doing something contrary to the world's understanding, they will try to send negative and a false sense of security down your path to cause you to doubt what you are speaking and walking according to the scripture. But a peace in Jesus Christ will pass all your understanding. It will be something in your spirit that confirms that you are on the righteous path. It fills you with love, peace and joy.

### KEY: DO NOT MOVE FROM "THE SECRET PLACE"

I learned to trust in the Word of God for my life no matter what things looked like, how they feel to my flesh, taste to my flesh, the way people treats me or what was said to me. I understand that it will all work in my favor, in God's timing. Gods' Word will not return void, if you hold onto the Word of God in your heart with the right intention and do not lose the heart of love. It is all about saving a lost soul and assisting the Spirit of God to bring them into the saving knowledge of our Lord and Savior, by being an example.

CHAPTER 3

ENTER IN TO RECEIVE

THREE TRUTHS
TEN ATTRIBUTES
SEVEN DEADLY SINS
SEVEN SINS GOD HATE

**THREE TRUTHS**

### Three truths I learned that will assist you in your Faith-Love-Walk:

**Seek the truth** = Seek first the kingdom and his righteousness and everything will be added unto you.

**Speak the truth** = Life and death is in the power of the tongue.

**Live the truth** = If we live in the Spirit, let us also, walk in the Spirit.

You get where God is, by living the Word of God in spirit and truth.

Satan cannot touch you behind the veil, and you cannot go behind the veil unless you are willing to bare all in spirit and truth.

> **KEY:** The veil is worn to keep something hidden for sacred reason.

God says to His people, "The veil keeps the revelation and illumination of His Word sacred." It is also symbolic to a world that tries to imitate God and live a life as though it can not be seen, but God said you are walking from a physical being, I can see all, I know all, and can unveil your life at anytime to whomever, but you cannot see me, because I am Spirit and you are not willing to bare all and be truthful from the heart, so the true you is hid in me and can not be revealed to you unless you walk in the Spirit of who I ordain you to be, before the foundation of this world and before you stepped into time. In me all things are hid, because it is a **"Secret Place."**

Understand that if you are not willing to walk in the Spirit and be truthful regarding all matters of the heart, you are just going through motions in this life, fulfilling temporary satisfaction with an end that is dead.

**Ask yourself, "Will God allow me in the kingdom with a heart that will do <u>whatever</u>?"**

God's Word is your substance for every situation. The proof will be you believed and trusted according to the scripture and it happens in God's timing. Just trust in God's Word and never doubt.

Faith is the substance of things hoped for, the evidence of the things not seen. Have faith-that-believes and trust what the Spirit of God speaks to the heart.

Don't become discouraged when truth is not revealed in your heart all at once. Keep meditating on the scriptures day and night, the more you meditate on what is written in the Word of God, the more you will begin to speak and do the Word of God under an anointing and inspiration of the Holy Spirit.

Just as the men of God in history wrote as the Holy Spirit inspired them, each small step you make in the Word of God from the heart, it will become you, and you to will be inspired to testify being a witness by telling someone or writing.

### THIS IS KNOW: IT IS LIKE FIRE
### SHUT UP IN YOUR BONES

True Faith that believes and trust will reshape your spirit until you are no longer a babe that is spiritually weak. You will become a strong saint, eating the meat of God's Holy Word, able to stand against the wiles of the devil and do the work the Lord has called you to do.

Rejoice in the Lord and speak forth the Word of God in Faith concerning circumstances that have bound you. Do not be a doubleminded man, because he is unstable in all his ways. **WHO CAN TRUST HIM?** To truly enlighten you, this man can not even trust himself, because he do not know his ways.

At this point, be truthful and honest with yourself. People must understand they can know the entire Word of God, but if they are not speaking and living the Word of God in spirit and truth, it is of no effect to you or others to whom you speak the Word of God too.

When you do not fully understand the Word of God, do not turn away. Be patient while you wait on the Lord to unfold it and work it out for your good. "Victory shall be yours," says the Lord. Keep reaching for the Word of God and allow your heart to be receptive to the Holy Spirit as he leads and guides you in spirit and truth concerning your situation.

We serve a revealing God, a God that takes the small things in this world to confound the wise. The God of Heavens takes failures and makes them successes.

**KEY:** "Those that wait upon the Lord shall renew their strength and mount up with wings like an eagle, run and not become weary walk and not faint." When you trust in the Word of God in spirit and truth, you feel like an eagle soaring in life situations that may come your way.

**TEN ATTRIBUTES**

**Ten attributes to assist your Walk to Spiritual Victory**

If you do not allow the Holy Spirit to direct you through these attributes in the way He knows best for you, you will only have temporary victory.

1. **Submission** = Submit to God, resist the devil and
                    he will flee. James 4:7

* Submit, yield, surrender in meekness and obedience to live and do the will of God. Resist the ways of the world that are contrary to the Word of God and the devil will flee from you.

* You must discern and understand to whom you are submitting. Know that everyone who says, "Lord, Lord..." may not have the Holy Spirit within him or her

* 1 Peter 2:13-20 reads, "Submit yourselves to every ordinance of man for the Lord's sake: whether it be to the king, as supreme: or unto governors, as unto them that are sent by him for the punishment of evildoers, and for the praise of them that do well. For so, is the will of God, that with well doing you may put to silence the ignorance of foolish men: as free, and not using your liberty for a cloak of maliciousness, but as the servants of God. Honor all men. Love the brotherhood. Fear God. Honor the king. Servants, be subject to your masters with all fear (respect); not only to the good and gentle, but also, to the froward(ungodly)

**KEY:** God knows that if you bring out any wrongful action of the person in authority, pride will get in their way and they will take up vengeance toward you by using others. God knows the imperfections in the authorities He put in place and will handle the charges of all whom execute judgment wrongfully, either in this life or in the life after.

2. **Sensitive** = For they know God's voice and a
                   stranger they will not follow, but
                   will flee from him, for they know

not the voice of strange.
John 10:3

- The sense or sensory. Marked by sensory perception, keenly, perceiving. Be sensitive to the Word of God. Exercise your sense daily in the Word of God. If a voice tries to direct or detour you from the will of God, you will be able to discern and not walk in that way, even if it cost you something.

- Jesus discerned the Pharisees, Saudraucees, and religious rulers. Jesus wants us to submit to his Holy Spirit and be sensitive to the Word of God to be likewise to discern the spirit that is within a person, to know and understand how to address the spirit.

- A person that says, "I know Him," but keeps not his commandments is a liar, and the truth is not in him. He is not sensitive to the Word of God.

- Be still, and know that I am God: I will be exalted among the heathen, I will be exalted in the earth

3. **Separation** = Come from among them (the world and its ways) and be separated, for I am the Lord thy God.

- Separate, part, divide, dismiss, to withdraw

- Ask Jesus for wisdom and revelation to discern between good and evil or a wolf in sheep's clothing, so that you will not walk in the way of these evil men because of an uncircumcised heart

- Study to show yourself approved unto God, a workman that needs not be ashamed, rightly dividing the Word of Truth.

4. **Obedience** = Will to do what one is told, submission to authority

- Obey my voice. I will be your God, and you shall be my people; and walk you in all the ways that I have commanded you, that it may be well unto you. Jeremiah 7:23

- We ought to obey God rather than men. Acts 5:29
  What manner of man is this, that even the winds
  and the sea obey Him? Matthew 8:27

- Obedience is better than sacrifice

5. **Sacrifice** = Offer the sacrifice of righteousness and
  put your trust in the Word of God. The
  act of offering your life for the life of
  Christ. You are letting go of the ways of
  the world for the sake of gaining
  something of more value and a greater
  weight of glory, which may not all be
  seen in this present world, but will be
  seen in its fullness in the new Heaven
  and new Earth.

- God said, "Gather my saints together unto me; those that
  have made a covenant with me by sacrifice." Psalm 50:5

- If I were offered upon the sacrifice and service of your
  faith, I am joy and rejoice with you. Philippians 2:17)

- Offer your sacrifice of righteousness and put your trust in
  the Lord. Psalm 4:5

6. **Switch** = A permanently changed life. Pull off the
  old man and put on the new man.

- To exchange, a redirecting of your life from evil
  (darkness) to good (light).

- The desire and ability to switch will determine your path
  in the new man.

- Be transformed by the renewing of your mind.
  Behold old things have passed away, all things
  have become new.

7. **Humble** = Be clothed with humility, for God
  resisteth the proud, and giveth grace
  to the humble. 1 Peter 5: 5-9

- Better it is to be of a humble spirit with the lowly, than to
  divide the spoil with the proud.

- Stay humble because pride bringth destruction. Being found in fashion as a man, Jesus humbled Himself and became obedient unto death, even the death of the cross.

- There will be many deaths to free will, but die to them, if you do not, you will open the door to whatever the world has to offer. Always apply God's Word to your life situation, even if you must humble yourself to do it.

8. **Love** = No matter what you are going through, love the Lord with all your heart, mind, soul and strength and love your neighbor as yourself.

- Strong feelings or affection for someone or something.

- Perfect love casts out fear. Love never fails. Love covers all sin. Love is of God and God is love.

- Jesus said, "With love have I drawn thee."

- We must possess the love Jesus speaks about (agape love) with an expectation in wonder, with an insatiable desire to bless someone unconditionally.

9. **Rest** = Inactivity after having labored in the Faith, relief from distress, a shelter. On the other hand, a place of stopping and relaxing to break from spiritual warefare and day to day responsibilities.

- When you have done all you can do according to the scripture, rest and have faith-that-believes and trust, that it will surely come to pass just has the Word of God has said.

- Jesus said, "Come unto me, all you that labor and are heavy laden and I will give you rest

- David said, "Therefore my heart is glad, and my glory rejoices: my flesh also, shall rest in hope.

- David said, "Rest in the Lord, and wait patiently for him; fret not yourself because of him who prospereth in his ways." Rest in the Lord in love, and fear not concerning the wicked devices of men. God is on your side.

10. **Peace** = Freedom from inner conflict; mentally and emotionally, absence or stopping of quarrels, the state of harmony between people, a spiritual tranquility, a quiet, calm or serenity.

- Depart from evil, and do well; seek peace, and pursue it. Psalms 34:14

- Thou will keep him in perfect peace, whose mind is stayed on thee because he trusteth in thee. Isaiah 26:3

- Be complete, Be of good comfort, be of one mind, live in peace; and the God of love will be with you. 2 Corinthinans 13:11. For he is our peace, who hath made both one, and hath broken down the middle wall of partition between us. Ephesians 2:14

**KEY:** These ten attributes must be your way of life in spirit and truth.

Submit, and be sensitive to the Word of God. Separate from your free-will. Obey the Word of God. Switch in your heart to hear and recieve the Word of God when spoken. Humble yourself in love. Rest in the Word of God. Live in the peace of God that passes all understanding.

Your faith must be tried in the refiner's fire. Jesus said, "Count it all joy when you are in diverse temptation; knowing this, that the trying of your faith works patience, but let patience have her perfect work, that you may be perfect and wanting nothing."

Understand your accuser will go to Our Father in Heaven to ask permission to try you, because he does not want you to take your rightful place in Kingdom Living in this present world. Satan is after your faith and praying lifestyle, he knows that prayer changes things and prayer will make a difference and through prayer you receive direction that has a greater weight of reward, if you do not lose heart.

## SEVEN DEADLY SINS

There are seven deadly sins. We must know of them and be aware of them.

The Bible says, **"Watch and Pray"**, be sober and vigilant; because your adversary the devil as a roaring lion walks about, seeking whom he can devour. Nevertheless, let us keep in our heart, it is a spirit that works in and through the people that are disobedient to the Word of God.

Satan will come after you with his demon spirit, bringing one of the seven deadly sins to try to deter you from God's righteous path. You must be cautious, but not paralyzed with fear in your spiritual walk, because along your path many devils will cross it to deter you from continuing in righteousness and holiness. Satan hates the existence of God's way of life in a world he calls his own.

Jesus said, **"Be ye holy for I am holy."** We serve a holy God. When you are filled with the Word of God the demon spirits cannot possess your spirit and soul or cause your body to follow in the way of one or all of the deadly sins.

Watch and pray, when a deadly sin is presented to you, it will not appear as though it is deadly. You must have your discernment turned on to see and hear what the spirit of God is saying to you.

### Beware of the seven deadly sins:

1.  **Lust** - A strong desire to possess or indulge in one's own selfish will. It includes lust of the flesh and lust of the eye. "Walk in the Spirit and you shall not fulfill the lust of the flesh" Galatians 5:16

2.  **Greed** - Eagerly desirous of any thing for any reason. "Who being past feeling, have given themselves over to lewdnes, to work all uncleanness with greediness" Ephesians 4:19

3. **Gluttony** - One who indulges in anything excessively. "Whoever keeps the law is a discerning son, But a companion of gluttons shames his father" Proverbs 28:7

4. **Pride** - Conceit, arrogance, high opinion of one's own importance. "For all that is in the world is the lust of the flesh, lust of the eye and the pride of life, and is not of Our Father in Heaven, but is of the world" 1 John 2:16

5. **Wrath** - Violent anger, a passionate act of punishment. "For the wrath of man worketh not the righteousness of God." James 1:20-27

6. **Slothful** - Lazy, inactive. "Because of laziness the building decays, and through idleness of hands the house leaks" Ecclesiastes 10:18

7. **Envy** - ill will, a feeling of discontent over the prosperity or success of another. "A sound heart is life to the body, but envy is rottenness to the bones" Proverbs 14:30

Satan will use one or more of these deadly sins to lure you away from the Kingdom of Heaven way of life.

Jesus says in bold letters, **"WATCH AND PRAY"**, Be sober and vigilant because your adversary the devil walks about like a roaring lion seeking whom he may devour.

**KEY:** Prayer gives you power to overcome satan's wicked devices.

Understand satan will try to weaken your level of faith, with an unworthy sense of thinking or steal your Joy that gives you the ability to continue in the Word of God.

Satan's spirit will flow in and through people who are willing to do evil or who have no clear understanding of the spirits (other names are foes, imps) lurking in the earth. These evil spirits are sent to test the level of your faith. Satan will watch you, setting a plan in motion to trap you in order to steal, kill, and destroy your faith in the Word of God. Do not take the bait.

Know that if you should unintentionally sin, the grace of God and his mercy is sufficient to see you through, if you repent quickly and turn from the wicked way.

However, should you sin tentionally, understand grace and mercy will see you through, but with a penalty attached.

## SEVEN SINS GOD HATES

There are seven sins that God hates. The seven sins that God hates are the seven deadly sins in which the enemy operates, in a very subtle manner. The bait will not appear as one of the seven deadly sins in the beginning. If they draw you in, exercise your faith in the Word of God. The Holy Spirit will guide you to the **"Secret Place."** Your eyes will open and you will see how subtle satan foes were in the process in attempting to pull you astray.

Let us look at the seven sins God hates and how they compare to the seven deadly sins.

**The seven sins God hates are listed in:**
      **Proverbs 6:16-19.**

1.   **A proud look.**
2.   **A lying tongue.**
3.   **Hands that shed innocent blood.**
4.   **A heart that deviseth wicked imaginations.**
5.   **Feet that are swift in running to mischief.**
6.   **A false witness that speaketh lies.**
7.   **He that soweth discord among brethren.**

Proverbs 6:20-24 reads, "My son keep thy father's commandment, and forsake not the law of thy mother: bind them continually upon thine heart, and tie them about thy neck. When thou goest, it shall lead thee, when thou sleepiest, it shall keep thee; and when thou awakes, it shall talk with thee. For the commandment is a lamp; and the law is a light; and reproofs of instruction are the way of life: to keep thee from evil women, from the flattery of the tongue of a strange woman. Lust not after her beauty in thine heart; neither let her take thee with her eyelids."

**KEY:**   If we keep the commandments of our Father-Which-Art-In-Heaven in our heart, we can keep from the sins of our forefathers. Remember, once God gives you the ability, you have the authority.

We have read of my experiences that has transfomed my life with a child like Faith to believe and trust, which has given me a relationship to know and understand who God is. Hopefully Wisdom, Faith and Love has gave you substance and encourage you to do the Word of God.

In our next few chapters we will begin to Build, Equip and Fortify our Spiritual house on the principles of God's Holy Word in order to go and do spiritual warfare in love in this present world.

God is a spirit and needs a vessel in which to operate in and through in this earth. Say to yourself, "Lord let your will be done in and through my life."

Now get ready. Get set. Let us Go in the Word of God! Walk and stand on the Word of God. Be mindful that Jesus commanded us to do all things through Christ Jesus. Be clothed in humility and the righteousness of Christ Jesus.

**KEYS:** Satan does not mind you standing on the premises of the Church, but he does not want you standing on the Promises from the Word of God.

Satan does not mind you coming in the building Of the Church, but he does not want you Building, Equipping and Fortifying in the Body Of Christ.

Satan does not mind you sitting in the pew in Church, but he does not want you to hear what Spirit says to the Church, being an overcomer To be granted to sit with Jesus on his throne Revelations 3:21

Satan does not mind you joining auxillaries in the Church, but he does not want you joining Together in the endeavor to keep the unity of the Spirit in the Bond of Peace. Ephesians 4:3

I will explain at the conclusion of this book how essential it is for you to have an understanding of how the Spirit communicates. The Word of God is Spirit, so you must continually build, equip and fortify yourself in the Word of God day by day in order to become who God destined you to be. Having your sensory exercised to communicates from spirit to the soul, in order for the body to respond in a Christ-like manner.

How can two walk together unless they agree? The enemy will come to try you, so exercise your faith. Do not play with or give space to those spirits that are operating contrary to the will of

God? They want to take control of your soul, to lead the body out of the will of God. The truth is, Satan knows he needs to bring you to a place where you are dead in your spirit, when you are dead in your spirit you cannot hear and understand the Word of God.

Obedience is better than sacrifice. If you disobey, you nullify your potential to please God. Nevertheless, since we serve a loving and gracious God that is rich in mercy and slow to anger, a sacrificial offering of righteousness will be accepted.

The word evil is from the enemy, but God said what man meant for evil, he will turn around for your good. So, turn evil around in your life. 'Evil' turned around is 'live.' You will live in spite of evil tatics, if you turn it over to Jesus. Jesus came to give life more abundantly.

Now we are embarking upon vital chapters to prepare your temple for Building, Equipping, Fortifying for Kindom Living to be in the earth. Here is an important key to grasp before we begin the remaining chapters.

Examine your motives in every word and deed. Be sure there's no motive, but to do the will of God in love toward all mankind. Keep in your heart with all diligence, because out of it flows the issues of life.

You need to possess and understand "Faith-that-believes and trusts in the Word of God, receives the Promises of God."

If there is any unforgiveness or bitterness concerning anyone or anything, please stop here and ask the Lord to create in you a clean heart and renew a righteous spirit in you. God says, "If any man has anything against his bretherning leave your gift at the altar and go make amends with your brother."

I Speak Boldly and with the Authority of God, that if you follow the principles found in the Word of God pertaining your situation in this life, it will bring love, peace, joy, an abundate life and give you the ability to love all men unconditionally.

**KEY:** In a quiet still place ask yourself and be honest: What or who are you hungering and thirsting for in this present world? Is it taking you away from the principles in God's Holy Word?

This book has been inspired by God to bring his children to a state of mind in their heart to see life through the life of Christ.

It is essential that you make changes and adjustment in your life to move in the direction that has been ordained for you before the foundation of the earth and before you stepped into time, to recieve life more abundantly.

**CHAPTER 4**

**ENTER IN TO
BUILD IN THE MOST
HOLY FAITH**

## BUILD IN THE MOST HOLY FAITH

In this chapter you will see the phrase, "Faith-that-Believes and Trusts". In order to have Faith-that-Believes and Trusts in the Word of God, you must possess child-like faith.

Romans 10:10-13,17 reads, "For with the heart man believes unto righteousness; and with the mouth confession is made unto salvation." For the scripture says, "Whosoever believes on Him shall not be ashamed. For there is no difference between the Jew and the Greek: for the same Lord over all is rich unto all that call upon Him. For whosoever shall call upon the name of the Lord shall be saved. So then, faith comes by hearing and hearing by the Word of God."

In other words, Salvation is as close as a spoken word out of a sincere heart. Understand, we are in the end times and there will be ciricumstance that will turn for the worse and people will let us down, but you must have Faith-that-Believes and Trust the Word of God, if you want to see anything from the Word of God come to pass in your life. God will not fail you and God's Words will not return void.

Many people say they have Faith-that-Believes the Word of God, but they do not truly trust the Word of God, this is why they are not doers of the Word of God.

People do not understand that trust comes from the heart and since many cannot operate from the heart with matters, they will not have the ability to walk in or stand on what the Spirit of God is speaking in their life situation.

Psalm 39:1-7, "I said, I will take heed to my ways that I sin not with my tongue: I will restrain my mouth with a bridle, while the wicked is before me. I was dumb with silence, I held my peace, even from good: and my sorrow was stirred. My heart was hot within me, while I was giving myself quiet reflection the fire burned: then spoke I with my tongue, Lord, make me to know mine end, and the measure of my days, what it is; that I may know how frail I am. Indeed you have made my days as hand breadth, And my age is as nothing before you; Cerainly every man at his best is but vapor. Surely ever man walks about like a shadow; Surely they busy themselve in vain; he heaps up riches, And does no know who will gather them. And now Lord, what o I wait for? My hope is in you."

**KEY:** Psalm 40:1-5, "I waited patiently for the LORD; and he inclined unto me, and heard my cry. He brought me up also out of an horrible pit, out of the miry clay, and set my feet upon a rock, and established my goings. And he hath put a new song in my mouth, even praise unto our God: many shall see it, and fear, and shall trust in the LORD. Blessed is that man that maketh the LORD his trust, and respecteth not the proud, nor such as turn aside to lies. any, O LORD my God, are thy wonderful works which thou hast done, and thy thoughts which are to us-ward: they cannot be reckoned up in order unto thee: if I would declare and speak of them, they are more than can be numbered.

Once you pray these scripture with a sincere heart that trust God's Words, you will sense a lifting above your circumstances. But, be not deceived, any evil communication will corrupt the good manners in which the scripture has placed you.

God processed me before I went into battle in this present world in spiritual warfare in LOVE through the four attributes. I realized in my heart, God loves me because of the chastening I received while I was walking in darkness and coming into the light.

He tells us in Hebrews 12:7-14, "If you endure chastening, God deals with you as with sons; for what son is He whom the father chasteneth not? Nevertheless, if you were without chastisement, whereof all are partakers, then are you bastards, and not sons. Furthermore we have had fathers of our flesh that corrected us, and we gave them reverence: shall we not much rather be in subjection unto the Father of spirits, and live? For they verily for a few days chastened us after their own pleasure; but He for our profit, that we might be partakers of his holiness. Now, no chastening for the present seems to be joyous, but grievous: nevertheless, afterwards it yields the peaceable fruit of righteousness unto them that are exercised thereby. Wherefore lift up the hands that hang down, and the feeble knees; and make straight paths for your feet, lest that which is lame be turned out of the way; but let it rather be healed. Pursue peace with all men, and holiness, without which **no man shall see the Lord**.

**Here below are each of the attributes explained in seperate chapters, to prepare for Spiritual Warfare.**

**BUILD IN THE MOST HOLY FAITH** (to construct): The purpose of building in the faith; is for God to fill you spiritually to construct a spirit to withstand the storms in this life, with the ability to hold onto the Word of God, bringing you to a place where God's Word moves in and through the you fluently in this present world. **God is not going to <u>fill</u> anyone that does not first allow Him to <u>form</u> them.**

**EQUIP IN THE MOST HOLY FAITH** (to furnish, provide): Once formed in the Word of God, He will begin to fill and ground you in HIS words with the Fruit of the Spirit. While you are a newborn babe in the Word of God, growing up in his spiritual stature, God will shelter you from many trials and tests while He is equipping you.

**FORITY YOURSELF IN THE MOST HOLY FAITH** (make strong): Now that you have allowed God to form, fill and ground you in the Word of God with the Fruits of the Spirit, your trials and tests must come. You can not grow unless the proving and testing experiences come into your life, because you have changed through the call and now is challenged to be God's chosen vessel to be commissioned in this present world.

**DO BATTLE IN THE MOST HOLY FAITH** (fight, have an encounter with the opposing forces, do armed conflict with): Now, you can go to war. However, remember that the battle is not yours. It is the Lord's. So, <u>speak</u> the Word of God, <u>stand</u> on the principles from the Word of God, and have a faith that-believes and trusts the Word of God in Love. God's Word is firm and settled and will not return void. Move in the direction of the Word of God and you will be victorious in Christ Jesus.

**KEY:** Love, patience, and longsuffering with a humble heart will be the way to victory in Christ Jesus. I want you to know some demon spirits are so deeply rooted in a person's soul that they do not want to let go and come out of the physical being of that person. It takes time for the Word of God to work in and through their physical beings. When you are on the battlefield and struggling with faith-that-believes, understand and know that God knows it is hard for you to trust, so he will slowly fill you with what you need to build that strong back bone in Christ Jesus. Understand, Satan's spirit has your soul and mind which contains your emotions, thoughts and decision-making ability (or willpower) and he doesn't want to release them and the person don't want to let go because it feels good to the body, which is their reality. But continue to be an example in spirit and truth.

In order to build, let us get an understanding of faith. Faith is the substance (the physical matter or material, the basic or essential part) of things hoped for (desired, anticipated), the evidence of (proof, indication) things not seen. For by it the elders obtained a good report. Hebrews 11:1, 2.

In order for the elders to obtain a good report, they prayed in **F-A-I-T-H**, put their hope in God's Word and He was able to create an atmosphere that produced in the natural what they had prayed by faith.

**F = Fervent prayer**

**A = Access to our Father in heaven**

**I = Illumination of God's Holy Word**

**T = Trust**

**H = Holiness**

God desires fervent prayer; prayer that shows great intensity of emotion, enthusiastic, glowing communication, where his Words are spoken back to Him in faith for the right motives and reasons in a sincere heart.

## "The prayer of a righteous man avails much"

Abraham was justified by faith and it was counted to him as righteousness. If we believe, our faith will do the same. Trust and delight yourself in God, and He will give you the desires of your heart.

Since our flesh is at enmity (war) with God, our flesh will say, "Fear! Do not trust. Do not wait. If you do not act upon this matter now you will lose." The flesh wants it right now, but God says that those that wait upon Him shall renew their strength and mount up with wings like an eagle, run and not be weary, walk and not faint.

Faith says, "Believe, trust, don't doubt. Be patient my child, it's working in your favor."

"Victory is yours," says the Lord. Do not try to understand with your mind. God' ways will pass your understanding. Have faith that believes and trust out of a pure heart in the Word of God.

### Here are three keys to remember before you pray:

1.  Pray with clean hands and out of a pure heart. It is vital to a successful prayer life. You cannot expect God to answer your prayers if there is any unconfused sins in your life or if you are harboring an unforgiving spirit.

2.  Pray in faith, believing with your whole heart that God hears and answers prayer. God said, "If we have a mustard-seed of faith, we can say to the mountain be removed and cast in the sea."

3.  Anyone can pray, but only those who are walking by faith in obedience to the Word of God can expect to receive answers from their prayers.

Understand that there are degrees of faith. Jesus speaks of them in the Word of God. Below, are a few stories youcan read that will nourish to build your spirit and allow you to see your level of faith. Whatever level of faith you are operating in, God will see you through to another level, if just hold on to God's Word. He said He would never leave you nor forsake you. This is an overcoming way and we must overcome in these last days to do a greater work in Christ Jesus.

1.  Jesus rebuked the disciples saying, "O ye of little faith." Matthew 8;23-27

2.  He commended a Cananite woman, "O woman, great is thy faith." Matthew 15:21-28

3.  A centurion, Jesus said, "I found so great faith, no not in Israel." (Luke 7:1-10)

4.  Paul mentions faith the size of a grain of mustard seed that can remove mountains. Matthew 17:20

Faith in Jesus Christ is necessary for our salvation. "He that believes not shall be damned." Not just any kind of faith will bring salvation from sin. There are people that <u>hear</u> the Word of God, <u>say</u> they believe in the Word of God, yet reject it in their heart, which sets them in motion to make decisions out of their free will.

We read the story above to see the disciples did not place their faith in who God is, they focused on the circumstance and made it bigger than God, but the Cananite and the Centurion placed their Faith in who God is, because they undstood God was bigger than the circumstances they were facing. Paul is saying to us if we have a very small portion of Faith, trusting in God to produce the results, it shall be moved.

To get an understanding, allow me to speak briefly on doubting:

All the disciples said to Thomas, Jesus is alive, because Thomas had seen with his eyes Jesus lifeless body, he could not believe Jesus was alive. No matter what the disciples continued to say to him, he did not believe. Jesus had to come face to face with Thomas and allow him to touch the nail prints in the hand for belief to come into his heart. Mankind is this way today, it will take Jesus coming down from Heaven, and they see the nail prints, for belief to come into their hearts. True Christian understands, without Faith it is impossible to please God. So we continue in the way of the Bless Hope that is within our Heart, but knowing God desire for all men to be saved, he knows that many will chose their free will. However we must spread the Love of Jesus Christ in the earth to all man-kind.

God says in Proverbs 4:23-27, "Keep thy heart with all diligence: for out of it are the issues of life, put away from thee a froward mouth, and perverse lips, put far from thee. Let thine eyes look right on, and let thine eyelids look straight before thee, ponder the path of thy feet, and let all thy ways be established, turn not to the right nor to the left: remove thy foot from evil."

**KEY:**  The Word of God, without a shadow of doubt must be ground and firm in your heart for you to go in the direction and stay the course according to God's Word.

You are given the answer through the Word of God. The
Word of God takes you on a straight and narrow path
and few go on it. The Word of God will make the crooked way
straight. In other words, apply the Word of God from your heart
in any situation in your life, it will cause matters to straighten
out. "Remove thy foot." In addition, look straight, meaning keep
your eyes on Word of God way.

We know that foot is singular, i.e., and one. God already knows
we will struggle in our decision making, desiring the way of the
world versus God's will, which some call 'straddling the fence.'
However, you must remove that foot from the world, and places
our feet on the solid foundation, which is in Christ Jesus.

People truly know God's Word is best, but most are not built,
euipped, fortified to be strong enough in their inner man to go in
the direction of the Word of God which is profitable to them.

God says, "Choose this day whether you will serve God or Man."
We must come to a place in our life where we say, "For me to live
in Christ and die to free will is gain."

The Holy Spirit revealed to me that most people do not
live by the Word of God, or govern their lives by it because man
has not represented Jesus Christ in the spirit of truth in an
appropriate manner. They do not appreciate the Gospel. Neither
have they acquired a hunger and a thirst in their belly for the
Word of God.

I pray that you go in the direction of holiness, no matter what
you see or hear from believers or non-believers, Trusting in God's
Call to Holiness for your life. Understand that many people have
a form of Godliness, but deny the power thereof. Many people do
not believe there is a power that works in the earth against the
evil ones, but truly, there is.

Keep and understand in your heart, God is slow to anger, Rich in
Mercy, and Love, giving Grace, clothe you in Righteousness, and
will hold your hand.

He gives you the opportunity to repent (turn) from the
wicked way. Repenting quickly gives you the opportunity to be
connected in a place of peace on the job, in the home, at the
church or where ever you may go.

If you do not, repent quickly, you begin to slip further in

darkness in that place of your life. You see things happen in your life that are not so good, you will try to pull others with you, because pride will not allow you to speak truth concerning your evil ways, so you hold firm to darkness.

You might get by, but you will not get over to the next place in peace. Ephesians 4:17-19 reads, "This I say, therefore, and testify in the Lord, that you henceforth walk not as other Gentiles walk, in the vanity of their mind, having their understanding darkened, being alienated from the life of God through the ignorance that is in them because of the blindness of their heart; who being past feeling have given themselves over unto lasciviousness, to work all uncleanness with greediness."

The faith we are speaking of and living, is a saving faith. It is of one mind, one heart in love. It is a faith that trusts, a faith that obeys God's commands and believes in his promises no matter what the flesh signals. If we continue to follow the signal from the flesh, we will become spiritually dead. Since the Word of God is Spirit, and spiritually discerned, you will not be able to get an understanding of the Word of God, neither will you be able to retain the Word of God. It will become frustrating to hear the Word of God; therefore, the falling away from the Word of God comes in your life.

Since we are building a Holy Faith to be established in it. The Spirit of God has brought you this far to empower you in his principles to build your faith to a level where you have confidence in what you say and do concerning the Word of God.

**Genesis 2:7** reads, "And the Lord God formed man of the dust of the ground, and breathed into his nostrils the breath of life; and man became a living soul."

### DO YOU BELIEVE GENSIS 2:7?

Submit your whole being, in a posture of obedience and humility, to the one that breathe a breath of life for you to become a living soul. You will become sensitive to God's voice and readily to obey. You will then have the ability to separate yourself **In Love** from anything or anyone that is contrary to God's Word, because God's love will be drawing you to a safe and peaceful place. You will feel and sense his warm and caring love through his Word. You will become willing to sacrifice whatever is needed in order to continue on the paths of righteousness with faith-that-believes and trusts in the Word of God.

God's Word gives you the desire and ability to switch from the old man to the new man permanently, that you can walk in the newness in your life. God says to us, "Behold all things become new." Behold means to look, see, or in today's vernacular, "Check it out." Keep yourself humble, because you understand it is nothing you are doing but everything God's Word has given you the ability and authority to do. Remember you are walking by Faith, not by sight. You spoke it according to the Word of God and even if you can not see it, you understand it will be because "I AM" is not a man that shall lie, and his word will not return void. Do not murmur or complain. Just keep the faith-that-believes and trust. Do not lose hope, it will work for your good.

**KEY:** God created your heart to love unconditionally. You were wonderfully made in Christ Jesus to do a great good work in the earth. But you must understand, you were born into a world of sin and shaped in iniquity. The world will shape you to do the sin. It goes back to the scripture; they have a form of God, but deny the power thereof.

The world functions on see, feel, taste, physical hearing, touch, so if you should speak and do outside of what they call the normal, they will try to pull you back, because they have no faith that believes and trust in the Word of God. Many people in this world truly believe the power is in them, not understanding we are speaking of a Power that has Love and is never partial in his answers, but alway true to what he does and speaks to the heart.

I would like my readers to know and understand, man do have a man made power to make people life miserable, but if they should go in that direction for an unrighteous cause, they will surely suffer on the other side of their life and it could come back in their present life. Unless they come back to the person in this life and make a wrong right. As sure as the world revolve in a circle, in God's timing they will reap that unjust seed that they sowed in somone elses life. This is why you do not worry or fret, have Faith that believes and trust in the Word of God.

You have no reason to be proud. Why? You are clothed in humility, and with that comes a love that has a desire for all souls to be saved and set free from the wages of sin and death.

I pray that God will give you revelation knowledge of the scriptures that follow, in order to understand <u>who</u> you are and <u>whose</u> you are. My prayer and hope is these scriptures will give you confidences in Love, with the ability and authority to exercise your faith in liberty, and freedom in the spirit.

Understand, **"GOD IS"** and **"GOD IS"** in the right now of your life. God is no respecter of a person. God said, "You shall know the truth and the truth shall make you free." Make means to create or produce. In other words, the Word of God will create a new free man in Christ Jesus that will begin his work on the inside of you, so you will know in your heart without any doubt that:

### **"Who the Son sets free is free indeed."**

These scriptures are food for the spirit-man to build and produce a solid foundation in your spiritual walk.

**2 Timothy 2:10-16** reads, "Therefore I endure all things for the elect's sakes, that they may also obtain the salvation which is in Christ Jesus with eternal glory. It is a faithful saying: For if we be dead with Him, we shall also live with Him: If we suffer, we shall also reign with Him, if we deny Him, He also will deny us: If we believe not, yet He abides faithful: He cannot deny Himself. Of these things put them in remembrance, charging them before the Lord that they strive not about words to no profit, but to the subverting of the hearers. Study to show thyself approved unto God, a workman that needs not to be ashamed, rightly dividing the word of truth. But shun profane and vain babbling: for they will increase unto more ungodliness."

**Galatians 3:21-29**, reads "Is the law then against the promises of God? God forbid: for if there had been a law given which could have given life, verily righteousness should have been by the law. Nevertheless, the scripture has concluded all under sin that the promise by faith of Jesus Christ might be given to them that believe. Nevertheless, before faith came, we were kept under the law, shut up unto the faith, which should afterwards be revealed. Wherefore the law was our schoolmaster to bring us unto Christ, that we might be justified by faith. Nevertheless, after that faith is come, we are no longer under a schoolmaster. For you are all the children of God by faith in Christ Jesus. For as many of you as have been baptized into Christ have put on Christ. There is neither Jew nor Greek, there is neither bond nor free, there is neither male nor female: for you are all one in Christ Jesus. And if you be Christ's, then are you Abraham's seed and heirs according to the promise."

**Galatians 3:21-29** lets us know that before we had the faith in Jesus Christ that delivered us from the destruction of our free will, we were held captive in the world of sin by the lust of the flesh, lust of the eyes and pride of life, which is not of our Father in Heaven, but of the god of this humanistic world.

Believe me when I say there are some that desire what makes their body feel good and have not counted the cost. Nevertheless, thanks be to God for the way of escape from the wages of sin.

God reveals his nature to us, his will for humanity, his moral laws and his guidelines for living. I would like you to know that you cannot be saved by keeping the Old Testament law. We must have Faith that believes and trust in Jesus Christ, who can down through 42 generation made of the Word of God, took on the sins of man-kind and provided a way of escape from eternal death.

He spoke in Matthew 5:17, "Think not that I am come to destroy the law or the prophets: I am not come to destroy, but to fulfill. Therefore, we must do as Paul said, "Take off the old robe of law, and put on Christ's new robe of righteousness."

**2 Corinthians 4:13-18** reads, "We, having the same spirit of faith, according as it is written, I believed, and therefore have I spoken; we also believe, and therefore speak; knowing that He which raised up the Lord Jesus shall raise up us also by Jesus, and shall present us with Him. For all things are for your sakes that the abundant grace might through the thanksgiving of many rebound to the glory of God. For which cause we faint not; but though our outward man perish, yet the inward man is renewed day by day. For our light affliction, which is but for a moment, works for us a far more exceeding and eternal weight of glory; While we look not at the things which are seen, but at the things which are not seen: for the things which are seen are temporal; but the things which are not seen are eternal."

Here is the revelation for **2 Corinthians 13-18:**

sometimes you might feel  at the end of your rope of
hope, but know that Paul tells us that we are never at
the end of our rope of hope in the Word of God. Our bodies are
subject to sin and sufferings in this present world, but God will
never leave us nor forsake us, neither will the righteous seed beg
for bread. All our risks, humiliations persecutions, trials and test
are opportunities for Christ to demonstrate his presence and
power in and through us in this present world. When we seek
eternal things we have a greater weight of glory (achievement,
honor and prosperity) and will rejoice with jubilation.

In building in the Holy Faith you must present your body as a
living sacrifice, holy, acceptable unto God, which is your
reasonable service. By this, all men will know that Jesus is alive
and dwelling in you, and God truly comes to seek and save the
lost. God will reach to the highest mountain and go to the lowest
valley to bring you to the place He had predestined for you, if you
are willing.

Have faith-that-believes and trusts in the Word of God or you will
have a Faith that trust in your own words.

Let us proceed to the next place: **Equipping in the Word of God
by Faith!**

**CHAPTER 5**

**ENTER IN TO
EQUIP IN THE MOST
HOLY FAITH**

## EQUIP IN THE MOST HOLY FAITH

You must pray the scriptures with a heart that believes. This will equip you to seek the truth, speak the truth, live the truth and receive in the heart, line upon line, precept upon precept, glory to glory to walk by Faith to Spiritual Victory.

**Psalm 119:25-30** reads," My soul cleaves unto the dust: quicken thou me according to thy Word. I have declared my ways, and thou heard me; teach me thy statues. Make me to understand the way of thy precepts; so shall I talk of thy wondrous works. My soul melts in heaviness: strengthen thou me according unto thy Word. Remove from me the way of lying: and grant me thy law graciously. I have chosen the way of truth: thy judgements have I placed before you. I have stuck unto thy testimonies: O Lord, put me not to shame. I will run the way of thy commandments, when thou shall enlarge my heart."

**Psalm 119:33-40** reads, "Teach me, O Lord, the way of thy statues; and I shall keep it unto the end. Give me understanding, and I shall keep thy law; I shall observe it with my WHOLE HEART. Make me to go in the path of thy commandments; for in them do I delight. Incline my heart unto thy testimonies, and not to covetousness. Turn away mine eyes from beholding vanity; and quicken thou me in thy way. Establish thy Word unto thy servant, who is devoted to thy fear. Turn away my reproaches that I fear: for thy judgements are good. Behold, I have longed after thy precepts: quicken me in thy righteousness."

God desires you to receive each line of his word and apply the principles in your life daily so you can see the Glory of God fill those dead places in your life.

Allow me to share how the holy spirit spoke to me and processed me through the equipping to ensure I was firm and settled thoroughly in salvation.

1. **We need Salvation**: A DESIRE within that brings            an understanding of the Word of God to be delivered from the sins in this present world:

    • For the wages of sin is death; but the gift of God is eternal life through Jesus Christ our Lord. Romans 6:23

    • For the grace of God that brings salvation hath appeared

to all men. Titus 2:11

- For He said, I have heard thee in a time accepted, and in the day of salvation have I succored thee: behold, now is the accepted time; behold, now is the day of salvation. 2 Corinthians 6:2

I would like my readers to know what the Spirit spoke to my heart regarding sin and why it is so hard for people to let it go.

Many people stay in fellowship with people of a sinful nature by giving justification for committing sinful acts, and they themselves become dull and numb to the truth of God's Word.

Let us look at the word **SIN**. Understand that:

**S** = A false sense of **S**atisfaction

**I** = An **I**nternal signal to the body (i.e., to the unregenerate soul-man which has not been exercised by the Spirit of God)

**N** = The **N**onbeliever that receives the false Signal of satisfaction, goes in the direction to fulfill the lust of the flesh, the lust of the eye and the pride of life.

The objectivity of Satan is to bring temporal satisfaction to all non-believers and if possible to believers to keep them going in a direction that will take them far out in their free will, they will feel a false sense within as though there is no return (no hope) from the place they are in. But God, who is faithful, gracious and rich in mercy, slow to anger with those who call on Him, will come to rescue them whether they are at the highest mountain in sin or in the lowest valley in sin.

He understands that on both ends of the spectrum you feel the false sense as though there is no return. But understand in your heart the motto, "No Return" is man's law. It is not from God's Word. The Lord wants us to know in our heart, "He can bring you up out of an horrible pit, out of the miry clay, the mess you mad, and set your feet upon a rock, and established yours goings." Psalms 40:2

2. **Cost of Salvation:** Jesus paid the ultimate cost

- For when we were yet without strength, in due time Christ died for the ungodly. For scarcely a righteous man wills one die: yet peradventure for a good man some would even dare to die. Nevertheless, God commends his love toward us, in that, while we were yet sinners, Christ died for us. Romans 5:6-8

- Who was delivered for our offences, and was raised again for our justification. Romans 4:25

- Nevertheless, He was wounded for our transgressions, He was bruised for our iniquities: the chastisement of our peace was upon Him; and with his stripes, we are healed. All we like sheep have gone astray; we have turned everyone to his own way; and the Lord hath laid on Him the iniquity of us all. Isaiah 53:5-6

**KEY:** Count the cost of salvation and you will begin to see and understand in your heart, the price has truly been paid, you owe nothing, but will recieve bountifully and you will understand that you are truly loved by the Almighty God.

3. **Way of Salvation**: The DIRECTION to have life more abundantly

- Moreover it is said, believe on the Lord  Jesus Christ, and thou shall be saved, and thy house. Acts16:31

- But as many as received Him, to them gave He power to become the sons of God, even to them that believe on his name. John1:12

- For with the heart man believes unto righteousness; and with the mouth, confession is made unto salvation. For the scripture said, whosoever believes on Him shall not be ashamed. Romans 10:10-11

- The way is narrow and few go thereof, broad is the gate and many will follow that leads to destruction. Matthew 7:13,14

- Jesus said, "I am the way , the truth, and the life; no man come unto the Father, but by me. If you had known me, you should have known my Father also; and from henceforth you know him, and have seen him. John 14:6,7

4. **Joy of Salvation**: A DELIGHT that strengthens your spirit-man, and uplifts the soul of man and directs the body in love, peace and unspeakable joy.

- Whom having not seen you love; in whom, though now you see Him not, yet believing, you rejoice with joy unspeakable and full of glory. Receiving the end of your faith, even the salvation of your soul. 1 Peter 1:8-9

- My brethren, count it all joy when you fall into diverse temptations; Knowing this, that the trying of your faith works patience. James 1:2-3

- Thou wilt show me the path of life: in thy presence is fullness of joy; at thy right hand there are pleasures for evermore. Psalm 16:11

- Delight yourself in the Lord, trust in the Lord and He will give you the desires of your heart.

- These things have I spoken unto you, that my joy might remain in you, and that your joy might be full. John 15:11

**KEY:** Because all our dependencies on God, it does not matter how high or low our circumstance are, through Christ Jesus we will keep a level mind and a humble heart, because our life is intertwind with HIS, we will have confidence that through adversity he will not allow us to sink beyond what we can bare, and we will manage our prosperity in a heart without moving into deceptive highs. True Joy transcends the rolling waves of circumstances of life.

5. **Term of Salvation:** A CONVENANT or AGREEMENT between God and all man-kind.

- What agreement hath the temple of God with idols? For you is the temple of the living God; as God hath said, I will dwell in them and walk in them; I will be their God, and they shall be my people. Wherefore come out from among them, and be you separate, said the Lord, and touch not the unclean thing; and I will receive you and be a Father unto you and you shall be my sons and daughters, said the Lord Almighty. 2 Corinthians 6:16-18

- I will remember my covenant, which is between me and you and every living creature of all flesh; and the waters shall no more become a flood to destroy all flesh. Genesis 9:15

- How can two walk together unless they agree? Amos 3:3

- Now hath He obtained a more excellent ministry, by how much also He is the mediator of a better covenant, which was established upon better promises. For if that first covenant had been faultless, then should no place have been sought for the second. For finding fault with them, He said, Behold, the days come, said the Lord, when I will make a new covenant with the house of Israel and with the house of Judah: Not according to the covenant that I made with their fathers in the day when I took them by the hand to lead them out of the land of Egypt; because they continued not in my covenant, and I regarded them not, said the Lord. For this is the covenant that I will make with the house of Israel after those days, said the Lord; I will put my laws into their mind, and write them in their heart:  and I will be to them a God, and they shall be to me a people. And they shall not teach every man his neighbor, and every man his brothers, saying know the Lord: for all shall know me, from the least to the greatest. For I will be merciful to the unrighteousness, and their sins and their iniquities will I remember no more. Hebrews 8:6-12

- He has given meat unto them that fear Him: He will ever be mindful of his covenant. Psalm 111:5

**KEY:** Jesus came down through 42 generation brought the Convenant of Grace.  Jesus Christ forgives our sin Brings us to God through his sacrifical death to be Cleansed of sin.  What's so good about this Convenant, it comes freely.

6. **Act of Salvation:** It is the principles that guide your ACTION away from danger,

destruction, sin and death.

Verily, verily, I say unto you, He that hearth my word, and believeth on Him that sent me, hath everlasting life, and shall not come into condemnation; but is passed from death unto life. John 5:24

- Behold, I stand at the door and knock: if anyman hears my voice, and opens the door, I will come into Him, and will sup with Him and He with me. Revelation 3:20

**KEY:** If action is an effect produced by something, then we understand, when we hear the Word of God, have faith that believes and trust in our heart, we will act on God's principles and produce a lifestyle that delivers from sin and death. Jesus says, " No longer will I call you servants for a servant does not know what his master is doing; but I called you friends, for all things that I heard from My Father I have made known to you. You did not chose me, but I chose you and appointed you that you should go and bear fruit, and that your fruit should remain, that whatever you ask the Father in My name He may give you. These things I command you that you Love one another." John 15:15-17

### GUARD YOUR HEART, OUT OF IT FLOWS THE ISSUES OF LIFE.

**Life and death are in the power of the tongue**

### ASK YOURSELF: WHAT AM I SPEAKING OR ALLOWING TO BE SPOKEN IN MY LIFE?

7. **Seal of Salvation:** It's making an Impression on
Confirms the Truth

- In whom you also trusted, after that you heard the word of truth, the gospel of your salvation: in whom also after that you believed, you were sealed with the Holy Spirit of promise. Ephesians 1:13

- I give unto them eternal life; and they shall never perish, neither shall any man pluck them out of my hand. My

Father, who gave them me, is greater than all, and no
man is able to pluck them out of my Father's hand. My
Father an are one. John 10:28-30.

Do not grieve theHoly Spirit of God, by whom you
were sealed the day of redemption. Ephesian 4:30

- Nevertheless the solid foundation of God stands,
  Having his seal: " the Lord knows those who are His, " and
  "Let everyone who names the name of Christ" depart from
  iniquity  2 Timothy 2:19

**KEY:** The Holy Spirit speak to the heart and it is
Confirmed through Jesus.  So, step
out in faith and be doers of the Word of God.

Now that you are seal, let all bitterness, wrath,
Anger, and evil speaking be put away from you,
With all malice. And be kind to one another,
Tenderhearted, forgiving on another, even as God
In Christ forgave you. Ephesians 4:31,32

My hope in Christ Jesus, is that, at this point you are sure of
your salvation.

Now, let's begin to spiritually prepare the HEART (mind),
will and emotions in order to equip you with an
understanding of the whole Armor of God that you may
be able to stand against the wiles of the devil.

Understand there is a spirit in man and if you do not allow God
to inspire you with the knowledge of the **HOLY ONE**, the powers
of darkness will deceive, defile, deter, devour, and destroy every
good purpose in you.

**Proverbs 9:10** tells us, "The fear of the Lord is the beginning of
wisdom: and the knowledge of the Holy is understanding."

We need to be exposed first to a power that expresses itself in
more than self-pity:

- A power that searches the deep things of God
- A power that understand the Heart of the Holy Spirit.
  (The Holy Spirit will lead and guide you into all truths.)

- A power that exposes, that reproves, that convicts that

casts out demonic influences, demonic bands, and tormenting fears.

- How are they cast out? Through perfect love. 1 John 4:18 says, "There is no fear in love; but perfect love casts out fear: because fear has torment. He that fears is not made perfect in love."

God has given the saints and believers in the faith weapons to defeat territorial spirits. The four weapons are another part of the equipment you will need along with the armor of God in your spiritual walk.

- **The Word of God - Authority**
- **The Power of God -The Holy Ghost**
- **The Name of Jesus - The Word Made Flesh (our intercessor)**
- **The Blood of Jesus - Clean and pure blood that cleanses and washes away our sins**

Be sure each day of your life that you appropriate the Armor of God, because each piece protects you from the cunning craftiness of satan and his demonic forces in this present world. Saturate your mind with the Word of God and hide it in your heart that you might not sin against God.

Keep your heart and all thoughts fixed on the Word of God, understanding, if Jesus Christ suffered, then how can you escape suffering in this present world, knowing the letter of the law killeth, but the spirit gives life.

**KEY: THIS WORD OF GOD MUST BE REVEALED TO YOU BY THE SPIRIT, BECAUSE GOD IS SPIRIT**

Bring every thought into captivity and pull down every stronghold that exalts itself over the knowledge of God. Stay alert and vigilant, but not paralyzed with fear, because we should fear no man, but respect all men, and fear God only.

We serve a God that hopes all men come into the saving knowledge of Him, who sent his son that we might have life in a more abundant way.

In the midst of the moral filth in this world, always remember God's command, "Wherefore come out from among them and be

separate said the Lord, and touch not the unclean thing, and I will receive you. I will be a Father to you and you shall be my sons and daughters, said the Lord Almighty."
2 Corinthians 6:17, 18

The Christian life is a spiritual warfare. Your enemy is Satan (a spirit), the God of this humanistic world system. In Satan's army are legions of demons (or imps) that perform his will. This is why God inspired the writers of his Word to write in bold letters to capture your attention **"WATCH AND PRAY**," because your adversary goes about as a roaring lion to seek whom he may devour.

There are only two families in this world; the family of God and the family of Satan.

**1 John 3:8-15** reads, "He that commits sin is of the devil; for the devil sinned from the beginning. For this purpose the Son of God was manifested, that He might destroy the works of the devil. Whosoever is born of God does not commit sin; for his seed remains in Him: and he cannot sin because he is born of God. In this the children of God are manifest, and the children of the devil; whosoever does not righteousness is not of God, neither he that loves not his brother. For this is the message that you heard from the beginning, that we should love one another. Not as Cain, who was of that wicked one, and slew his brother. And wherefore slew he him? Because his own works were evil, and his brother's, righteous. Marvel not, my brother, if the world hates you. We know that we have passed from deat unto life because we love the brethren. He that loves not his brother abides in death. Whosoever hates his brother is a murderer: and you know that no murderer hath eternal life abiding in him."

The only way to defeat Satan and his legions of demons or imps, is to "Be strong in the Lord and in the power of God's might. Put on the whole armor of God, that you may be able to stand against the wiles of the devil."

There are seven spiritual pieces of the armor of God which must work in unity (seven is God's perfect number). Each piece is just as important as the others. Each piece is a source of power and protection to all the vital parts of a Christian Spirit in his spiritual walk. The seven pieces (Shield of faith, Helmet of Salvation, Breastplate of Righteousness, Buckler of Truth, Feet Shod with the Gospel of Peace, Prayer) will prepare you for a life

of spiritual warfare in love, which leads to victory.
The Lord says, **WE ARE NOT DEFEATED.**

**The first three prepare you for a Christian lifestyle:**

- **The shield of faith**
- **The sword of the spirit (Word of God)**
- **The helmet of salvation.**

**The second, three give you the ability to walk according to the Word of God:**

- **The breastplate of righteousness**
- **The buckler of truth**
- **Feet shod with the gospel of peace**

**The seventh piece is your communication to Our Father in Heaven, that gives you the assurance to stand:**

- **Pray**

The seventh piece, everybody forgets. It is not applied with the other pieces of equipment, but should be, because it is a vital and a critical piece for the fight. It is your communication through the Holy Spirit to Jesus Christ that leads with love to a safe, peaceful and victorious place in your life, with an assurance to stand.

I'm stopping here to inform you: if the direction you take does not bring peace or love in your inner man, yet you still walk in that direction, there must be something in you that is not Christ-like. You will need deliverance in that place of your life. God loves you so much that He will allow you to take paths in your life that are contrary to the Word of God in order to know the difference between His love for you and your love for yourself.

Believe me when I say that His love is greater and sweeter than the honey in the honeycomb. God's love for us reaches to the highest mountain and the lowest valley. I know this for myself, by working the Word of God.

At the end of this life no one will have an excuse as to why they did not choose God's way of life. He sends warnings or Godly counsel in all his children's paths.

Prayer will activate the Word of God for you to overcome struggles you are facing in your everyday life, and gives you strength to walk through the spiritual battles that has manifest in the natural.

Pray always with all prayer and supplication **[humbly]** in the spirit, watching thereunto with all perseverance and supplication for all saints.

Later, we will go into the meat (in depth) concerning the Armor of God, but for now, the Holy Spirit will minister through me the milk (the basics) of each piece of this equipment.

Understand you have been saved from sin and death when you accepted Jesus Christ as your Lord and Savior. Don't allow Satan's spirit to confuse you with evil thoughts. Hear God's Word and believe from your heart. Be prepared with the Word of God when temptation comes your way.

Count it all joy when you are in diverse temptations. It is just a test of your faith. Understand that you cannot grow unless these proving and testing experiences come into your life. Hold firm to the Word of God in your heart as you journey in your Christian walk and you will be able to draw upon God's aid, quickly.

Move forward in the Word of God with Love, Courage, Confidence and Faith, Trust, and always allow God's Word to go ahead of you. No matter how mature you are in the Word of God or how well developed your faith, never think for a moment that you need the support of God's Word any less. The truth is, you need the Word of God even more.

Allow me to minister the milk regarding the Armor of God in order that you grasp an understanding on how to walk with the whole Armor of God into Spiritual Victory in this present world.

**KEY:** Vision of this Armor. We know that before a soldier is sent out onto the battlefield he must learn, get to know, have an understanding and love every piece of equipment he has been given, in order to <u>survive</u>

## HELMET OF SALVATION

A covering of hard material, often metal, designed to protect the head in warfare. God portrays the helmet of salvation; like **HIMSELF**, a hard substances; that protects the head which holds the mind that contains our thinking processes with the saving knowledge of Christ, God is Rock solid.

Why metal? God understands this substance is very hard and can only be destroyed by very high temperatures. The enemy does not have a weapon powerful enough to penetrate the helmet of salvation, unless you surrender by taking off the saving knowledge of Jesus Christ

Stay committed to God's Holy Word, do not take off the helmet of salvation. No matter what is going on around you or in your life, have faith-that-believes and trust that God works all things together for the good of those who love Him and are called according to his purpose. The battleground is in your mind, the enemy knows it, this is why he tries to attack the mind with many dead thoughts, for you to take the wide road.

**KEY:** Keep the Helmet of Salvation on the head having faith-that-believes and trust God for what you prayed according to the Word of God. You will have the ability and power to bring every thought into captivity and pull down strongholds that come against the knowledge of God. The enemy attempt is to try your Faith in Salvation, to get you to doubt in whom you believe and turn

away from the Jesus who you confessed your sins
to, and who you accepted as your Lord and Savior,
with a desire to believe and trust in the Word of
God.

## SWORD OF THE SPIRIT

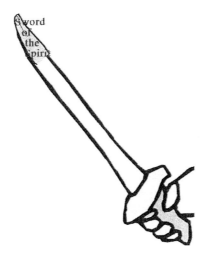

The sword of the Spirit is the Word of God. A sword is put into action to ward off satanic thrusts. In love, you counteract your enemy with God's Word.

Allow me to take a moment to speak to your heart, the way it was spoken to me concerning the Sword of the Spirit, which is the Word of God.

I was at work, walking through the plant when one of the guys was using what is called a diamond-edge circular blade to cut concrete. The dust from the blade was pure white, like snow. I ask him, how does this equipment work on this dirty concrete and I not see the dirt in the snow like particles.

He said, it is the diamond in the blade with water that gives it the ability to cut through the concrete making the particles appear pure.

After this guy finish, I walked away and the Spirit of God began to speak to my heart. Phyllis, am I not the fountain of life that springs up to every lasting life, I said yes, when you activate the Sword of the Spirit is not the Word of God water that quenches your thirst?, I said yes, did   not I say the Word of God is quick and sharper than a two edge sword, I said yes. Do diamonds have a beautiful shine? I said yes. The Spirit spoke, I AM is the diamond that is in the Sword of the Spirit that can not be seen unless Love is there. "I AM" cuts through the stony hearts of man, seperating the bone(True) from the marrow(fake) for people to see the intent of their heart, even though their sins are dirt, in me they will become pure and white as snow."

## SHIELD OF FAITH

Faith is your shield for the body. By it, you are able to quench all the fiery darts of the wicked ones.

When you stop having faith-that-believes and trust in the Word of God, you have laid the Shield of Faith down, the enemy's knows it. The enemy will begin the fiery darts attack to weaken your Faith, it will penetrate the breastplate of righteousness, to try to get you to take off what is righteous in your life.

## BREASTPLATE OF RIGHTEOUSNESS

We wear Christ's imputed righteousness formed in us by the Spirit of God. This is the sure protection of the heart from satanic attacks.

When you stop operating in the righteousness of God, the enemy will hit you in the heart, because you have dropped the Shield of Faith and you are not operating in what is the righteousness of God.

**KEY:**  Satan knows and believes the Word of God and will keep trying you until he fines a weak place in your life. Satan will continue hit that weak place in your life until you give evidence of a firm foundation on the Word of God. Nevertheless, never take Breastplate of Righteousness off in any area of your life.

DO NOT GIVE UP OR GIVE IN; CONTINUE TO COUNTERACT WITH THE WORD OF GOD. " BE STRONG IN THE LORD AND IN THE POWER OF GOD MIGHT."

## WE ARE ON THE BATTLEFIELD OF ETERNAL LIFE

## BUCKLER OF TRUTH

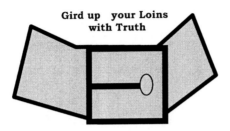

**Gird up  your Loins
with Truth**

Truth is at the center (Heart) of God's Word. The buckler of truth holds the Breastplate of Righteousness in place and supports the Sword of the Spirit.

Once you let go of the truth in the heart, the Breastplate of Righteousness falls off and the sword of the Spirit do not fit properly. In other words, your truth is deceptive and wavering. You are walking in your righteousness, which is the way a way that seems right unto man, but the end is destruction, which can end in eternal death.

The enemy knows, your words mean nothing. Now you are open target to the world way of life and you will be tossed to and fro truing to get someone to side with your deceptive wavering ways.

### Feet Shod with the Gospel of Peace

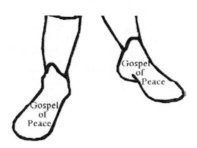

The Gospel prepares you to be a good soldier by giving you Love with inner peace and victory over Satan and his foes.

The Gospel of Peace is the life of Jesus Christ and the teachings of Jesus and his apostles. It is the absolute truth. Do not leave off the Gospel of Peace, because without it, your way will be dissatisfaction and confusion.

# PRAYER

We must keep our heart pure and our hands clean before the Lord. Understanding in our heart, 1 Thessalonians 5; 15-23, See that none render evil for evil unto any man: but ever follow that which is good, both among yourselves, and to all men. Rejoice evermore. Pray without ceasing. In everything give thanks; for this is the will of God in Christ Jesus concerning you. Quench not the Spirit, Despise not prophesying. Prove all things; hold fast that which is good. Abstain from all appearance of evil. And the very God of peace sanctify you wholly: and I pray God your whole spirit and soul and body be preserved blameless unto the coming of our Lord Jesus Christ.

Prayer is the appropriation of all the believer's resources in Christ in this present world. It is the actual purpose of strength, power and direction in Christ Jesus. In other words, without prayer you have no power or direction.

Last, but not least, I must say again, before you go out onto the battlefield wearing the Armor of God, allow God's Spirit to fill you with the Fruits of the Spirit and allow the fruits to work in and through you fluently; not artificially, but genuinely. The fruits of the spirit are essential on the battlefield in the present world we live in today.

Have faith-that-believes and trust that He who began a perfect work in you, shall fulfill it to the end.

In **Colossians, 4:12** we are told that someone is praying for you.

"Ephaphras, who is one of you, a servant of Christ, salutes you, always laboring fervently for you in prayers so that you may stand perfect and complete in the will of God."

**In 2 Timothy 3:17** we are told, "That the man of God may be perfect, thoroughly furnished unto all good works."

With all diligence, add to your faith, virtue; and to your virtue, knowledge; and to your knowledge, temperance; and to your temperance, patience; and to patience, Godliness; and to your Godliness, brotherly kindness; and to your brotherly kindness, charity. Having the assurance you are thoroughly furnished with the Fruits of the Spirit.

For if these things be in you and abound, you shall neither be barren, nor unfruitful in the knowledge of our Lord Jesus Christ. But he that lacks these things is blind and can not see afar off and hath forgotten that he was purged from his old sins. Wherefore the rather, brethren, give diligence to make your calling and election sure: for if you do these things, you shall never fall: For so, an entrance shall be ministered unto you abundantly into the everlasting kingdom of our Lord and Savior Jesus Christ. Wherefore I will not be negligent to put you always in remembrance of these things, though you know them and be established in the present truth." **1 Peter 1:5-12**

- **LOVE / Charity**
- **PEACE / Knowledge**
- **GOODNESS / Virtue**
- **KINDNESS / Brotherly Kindness**
- **FAITHFULNESS / Faith**
- **JOY / Godliness**
- **SELF-CONTROL / Temperance**
- **GENTLENESS / Godliness**
- **PATIENCE / Patience**

It's essential to read and meditate on the promise of the Spirit in John 14:9-21, until it consumes the spirit within and gives the assurance to walk in the principles of God in Love, Faith and confidence in Him, who has done a good work in you. Understanding, if you ask anything according to HIS will, HE hears us. Moreover, if you understand He hears, whatever you ask, you understand God will answer. Therefore do not be unwise in your own eyes, but understand what the will of the Lord is **in your heart**.

In **Genesis 5:21-24** we are told, "Enoch walked with God; and he was not; (not = in no way, to no extent, refused) for (for = instead, because, since, in honor) God took him away."

This scripture clearly shows us that Enoch was not in no way functioning from flesh desires, but dedicated to the spirit within him, which was God. Enoch character was manifested in the likeness and image of God as he walked with God and God took him away.

Do not be alarmed. Understand in your heart many people in the churches will reject holiness and try to keep you from walking in the sanctification and purity of God's Word. People make statements such as: you are only human, we have all fallen short, grace and mercy is here to save us.

Nevertheless, understand that grace is a gift you do not deserve. It is <u>not</u> here for you to fulfill the lust of your flesh, lust of your eyes or pride of life Yes, we stumble along the way, James 4:17 says, "Therefore to Him that knows to do well and does it not, to Him it is sin."

I would like to give a clear understanding of the act of actually doing the sin: The chastisement from the Lord for sins, does not happen at death, but over the course of your life while on this earth. If you should not heed the warning you shall reap an eternal spiritual death for the soul, and the body returns to the dirt of the ground.

Therefore, to know the scripture and do it not, you will be     whip with many strips. The whipping of many strips will be satan and his foes having the opportunity to trample in your life with the world's standards.

**KEY: YOU ARE THE ONLY ONE THAT CAN OPEN THE DOOR TO SATAN AND HIS FOES.**

If your testimony is true that God has delivered you from wages of sin.

**Why then be a dog that returns to his vomit?**

**Think of what you are showing others?**

**Is the Word of God, of no effect? <u>GOD FORBID!</u>**

I pray and hope my readers at this point of the book have a foundation built and equipped, to stay steadfast, unmovable in the doctrine of faith.

We over come, by the blood of the Lamb and the word of our testimony.

I know this for sure, this is an overcoming way of life, and you must live it, day by day. Some people must live it, hour by hour, because they have not processed the Word of God in their heart to live it in a natural way throughout the course of their day. They have no understanding of repentance that turns you from the wicked way.

Be thankful that God chose you to be in his army, know and understand Him as Lord and Savior, who is the head of your life and saves you from a world systems gone bad.

Thank Him for his Holy Word that by it you may grow spiritually strong and live a life worthy of HIS most precious sacrifice, Jesus Christ.

Let us proceed in fortifying ourselves in the Word of God with a faith-that-believes and trusts in order that we might receive the Promises of God.

**CHAPTER 6**

**ENTER IN TO
FORTIFY IN THE MOST
HOLY FAITH**

## FORTIFY IN THE MOST HOLY FAITH

Let us continue by fortifying in the most holy faith. Fortify means to make strong, to strengthen by military works against attacks.

We add vitamins and minerals to our system to help keep the body in good health. Let us add God's wisdom, knowledge, and spiritual understanding to keep strong, so we can spiritually stand against the wiles of the devil in this present world.

At this point, I would like you to know that you can do all the building and equipping of a spiritual house in Jesus Christ, but if you do not have faith with a strong desire within, possessing the four attributes listed below that will fortify you, you can easily go into a backslidden state of mind.

**Read what the spirit has to say about the woman at the well in John 4: 7-42, only then will you clearly see:**

- Your thirst has to be aroused for the Word of God only, no compromise
- Your thirst must transcend anything else. There is nothing greater than doing the Word of God for your life
- You have to want the Word of God in life's situations and nothing else. Understanding there is nothing better than applying God's principles in your life and walking them out.
- Your heart and mind set must be lifted above what people think or say.
- You must be at a place in your life, where you care less of people's opinions and their gossip.
- Youn must posses God's attribute (Love) and know at all times HIS attribute is HIS attitude that is an ACTION.

Read and Meditate on the scriptures below to assist in the transformation from the old man and fortifying the new man in Christ Jesus.

- **Colossians 1: 9-13**, "For this cause we also since the day we heard it, do not cease to pray for you and to desire that you might be filled with the knowledge of his will in all wisdom and spiritual understanding; That you might walk worthy of the Lord unto all pleasing, being the Lord unto all pleasing, being fruitful in every good work and increasing in the knowledge of God; strengthened with all might according to his glorious power, unto all patience and longsuffering with joyfulness; giving thanks unto the Father which hath made us meet to be partakers of the inheritance of the saints in light: who hath delivered us from the power of darkness and hath translated us into the kingdom of his dear son."

- **Psalm 27:1-4**, "The Lord is my light and my salvation: whom shall I fear? The Lord is the strength of my life; of whom shall I be afraid? When the wicked, even mine enemies and my foes, came upon me to eat up my flesh, they stumbled and fell. Though a host should encamp against me, my heart shall not fear: though war should rise against me, in this will I be confident. One thing have I desired of the Lord, that will I seek after; that I may dwell in the house of the Lord all the days of my life, to behold the beauty of the Lord and to inquire in his temple."

- **Colossians 3:5-10**, "Set your affection on things above, not on things on the earth. For you are dead and your life is hid with Christ in God. When Christ, who is our life, shall appear, then shall you also appear with Him in glory. Mortify, therefore, your members which are upon the earth, fornication, uncleanness, inordinate affection, evil concupiscence and covetousness, which is idolatry: for which thing's sake the wrath of God comes on the children of disobedience: in the which, you also walked some time, when you lived in them. Now you also put off all these; anger, wrath, malice (spite, desire to injure another), blasphemy (to mock, action concerning God with no true fear), filthy communication out of your mouth. Lie not one to another, since you have put off the old man with his deeds; and have put on the new man that is renewed in knowledge after the image of Him that created him."

- **Ephesians 4:17-24**, "This I say, therefore, and testify in the Lord, that you henceforth walk not as other Gentiles walk, in the vanity of their mind. Having the understanding darkened, being alienated from the life of God through the ignorance that is in them because of the blindness of their heart: Who being past feeling have given themselves over unto lasciviousness, to work all uncleanness with greediness. But you have not so, learned Christ: If so, be that you have heard Him and have been taught by Him, as the truth is in Jesus: that you put off concerning the old man, which is corrupt according to the deceitful lusts; and be renewed in the spirit of your mind; and that you put on the new man, which after God is created in righteousness and true holiness."

- **2 Peter 1: 3, 4**, "According as his divine power has given unto us all things that pertain unto life and Godliness, through the knowledge of Him that hath called us to glory and virtue: whereby are given unto us exceeding great and precious promises: that by these you might be partakers of the divine nature, having escaped the corruption that is in the world through lust."

- **Colossians 3:12-17**, "Put on therefore, as the elect of God, holy and beloved, bowels of mercies, kindness, humbleness of mind, meekness, longsuffering; Forbearing one another and forgiving one another, if any man have a quarrel against any: even as Christ forgave you, so also do you. And above all these things put on charity,which is the bond of prefects. Moreover, let the peace of God rule in your hearts, to which also you are called in one body; and be you thankful. Let the word of Christ dwell in you richly in all wisdom; teaching and admonishing one another in psalms and hymns and spiritual songs, singing with grace in your hearts to the Lord. In addition, whatsoever you do in word or deed, do all in the name of the Lord Jesus, giving thanks to God and the Father by Him.

As you view our old nature verse the new nature, know that every thought that comes will be through the entrance of your mind. An ungodly spirit will bring every kind of thought that is contrary to the Word of God. Sometimes the thoughts can be strong and persistent. This is why we must bring the soul and body under subjection to the Word of God. You do this by studying the Word of God to show yourself approved, a workman that can rightly divide the Word of Truth. Your heart will be strong enough to put the soul and body in submission to the Spirit.

Function from the standpoint that God will protect you just as the children of Israel were protected. The peace of God, which passes all understanding, shall keep your heart and mind through Christ Jesus.

**KEY:** Keep in mind that our greatest weakness in the old man is truly our greatest strength in our new nature in Christ Jesus. Be clothed in the new nature. When you understand where you get your power, that will be your greatest strength.

**Put off the old man (i.e., the power of darkness).**

**Put on the new man (i.e., the power of light)**

**Mortify the old man! Kill it outright- in order to fortify the new man.**

Our flesh wants comfort and is never satisfied, but **do not give way** to the yearning from the flesh.

God gives us power over our flesh as we yield to HIS Holy Word. The Holy Ghost is our comforter.

## HOLINESS IS A CALLING

Only those who put forth effort, will become new in Christ Jesus.

**Live a life of Christ and he will be:**
- **Your Bread of Life**
- **Your Tree of Life**
- **Your Water of Life**
- **Your Fountain of Life**
- **Your Crown of Life**
- **He will be the Spirit that gives you Life**

So therefore, walk in the Newness of Life in Christ Jesus.

Read and meditate on these scriptures:

- **Colossian 3:5-9,10-17**
- **Ephesians 4:17-22**

At this point, I must stop again and ask you to examine your life truthfully.

Is there anything or any situation concerning your life that does

not represent the Life of Jesus Christ? If you answer yes, let us
start there, because you need a starting point, and many times
it's one point at a time.

Let us pull off the old sinful nature; put on the new nature that is
in Christ Jesus. If we walk in the light, as He is in the light, we
have fellowship one with another and the blood of Jesus cleanse
us from all unrighteousness. You will feel a great weight
removed, from the inside to the outside, when you truly apply the
principles of God to your life and walk them out in spirit
and truth.

**KEY:** You have a friend, Christ Jesus who sticks closer
than a brother.

Here are names of God to assist in fortifying in a Holy Faith-that-
Believes and Trusts in the Word of God. I have found in my life
experiences, in times of trouble, trials, or testing, I call on HIM,
he will hear and answer.

- **The Son of God**
- **The Word made flesh**
- **The Way, the Truth and the Life**
- **Holy One of Israel**
- **Horn of my salvation**
- **Wonderful Counselor**
- **Redeemer**
- **Faithful and True**
- **Righteous Judge**
- **Prince of Peace**
- **Bread of Life**

When you call God by the above names, it's an up lifting within
and gives you an inner strength where you can hardly describe in
words on how it is directing you, until it is over, then it becomes
a living testimony.

Now ask yourself: "Have I taken the steps of Faith-that-Believes
and Trusts in the Word of God in order to receive Jesus Christ,
as my Personal Savior?"

Jesus said, "Behold I stand at the door and knock: if any man
hears my voice and opens the door, I will come in to him and sup
with him and he with me." Revelation 3:20

What door? The door is your heart. I would like to enlighten you that Satan's spirit can not enter your heart. He can only come through the entrance of your mind. God created your heart only to love and when you began to use your heart for anything other than love, you become sick in your mind with your throught process. In some instances, you end up with an internal illness, because you are harboring something that God did not create the heart to hold onto.

You carry an attitude that the outcome of what you do or say according to God's Word is **NOT** important enough to change the situation, because there is no power to turn circumstances in your favor, because you are looking from the physical. God's Words will not return **VOID.**

Who Knocks? God's knock with his Word on your heart in Love, it is as sweet as the honey in the honeycomb, and it brings deliverance, healing, blessings, and miracles.

What opens the door? When you hear God's Word, you respond with Faith-that-Believes and Trusts from the heart, Jesus comes in sups with you, because you open the door to let his Spirit be free in the earth.

If Satan's spirit knocks it will be at the entrance of our mind, he will try to deceive you into following a twisted thought in your situation. Satan sits in the seat of your mind trying to convince you to accept twisted thinking. Satans thinking carries no compassion, remorse, truth, consideration, unconditional love, but there is greed and selfishness. It blinds true love and muffles the sound of the Word of God knocking on the door of your heart. God, therefore, cannot come in and sup with you and you are definitely not supping with Him, because you are heartless at this place in your life, listening to the sound and feeling from your physical being.

When Jesus came out of the wilderness after forty days and nights, the tempter came to Him with a twisted version of the Word of God. The scripture was spoken to Jesus in a selfish manner, but Jesus understood Our Father in Heaven commands and blessings for all man-kind, and does not come by showing off **GOD'S POWER.**

**KEY:** Jesus understood God loves all mankind and is not respect of a person. It is not about what you do to receive great gifts, it is about your heart condition in what you are doing in receiving great gifts. Jesus understood, Our Father in Heaven does not place you in hight places to look down on other or succumb to their ways, but to be an example in spirit and truth.

### Beware of satan spirit that is lurking in the earth

God speaks to you only through his Word. "It is easier for Heaven and earth to pass, than one tittle of the law to fail." Be open to everything, but attached to nothing, except the principles and moral standards in God's Holy Word. Jesus tells us, "His sheep know his voice and a stranger they will not follow."

Opening the door is having a heart that can hear God speak and act on what is spoken. The Holy Spirit will be the teacher, so spend time in the Word of God, building, equipping and fortifying for Kingdom Living in the earth.

### KEY: THY KINGDOM COME THY WILL BE DONE IN THE EARTH AS IT IS IN HEAVEN.

Speak and keep these ten great truths in your heart, because in this life you will need to know and accept them without any doubt.

1. I am God's child, a child of the King.
2. I have a changed life through Christ Jesus.
3. I am secure in Christ Jesus
4. He is my refuge and strength, a present help in times of trouble.
5. I know my Heavenly Father cares about me at all times.
6. God says, cast my cares on Him, for He cares for me.
7. I have a good example, Jesus Christ "Be ye Holy, for I AM Holy."
8. I have a forever-friend. He no longer calls me a servant, but a son.
9. I have the Holy Spirit within me, "Be filled with the Holy Spirit."
10. I am the Righteousness of God.

**HOLINESS** – (holy - morally and spiritually pure, perfect, sacred, consecrated). You are called to holiness before you are called to any office in the Body of Christ.

## The gifts are without repentance

I would like to stop to allow you to see the difference between God calling and God-called. If God is calling you, the telephone is ringing but you have not answered. If God called, you have answered and accepted the assignment and it is sealed in Christ Jesus.

Thy testimonies are very sure: Holiness becomes thine house, O Lord forever. (Psalm 93:5)

God tells us through David, in Psalms 19: 7-14, "The law of the Lord is perfect, converting the soul: the testimony of the Lord is sure, making wise the simple. The statues of the Lord are right, rejoicing the heart: the commandment of the Lord is pure, enlightening the eyes. The fear of the Lord is clean, enduring forever: the judgements of the Lord are true and righteous altogether. More to be desired are they than gold, yea, than much fine gold: sweeter also than honey and the honeycomb. Moreover, they warn thy servant: and in keeping of them, there is great reward. Who can understand his errors? Cleanse thou me from secret faults. Keep back thy servant also from presumptuous sins; let them not have dominion over me: then shall you be upright and you shall be innocent from the great transgression. Let the words of my mouth and the meditation of my heart be acceptable in thy sight O Lord, my strength and my redeemer."

Keep this in your heart: God's statutes stand firm. Holiness adorns your house for endless days.

**Statutes = representation (firm), hard, solid, stable**
**Adorn = to beautify, dignify**
**Endless = without end**

**KEY:** In representing the Word of God you must be stable, firm, settled and beautiful without an end to what God will make happen for you in this life and the afterlife.

The Lord said, "Be ye holy for I am Holy." (1Peter 1:13-16) Be complete in your walk with the Lord Jesus Christ. Go all the way with Jesus and have no doubt whose child you are.

Read and meditate on these scriptures and receive them in your heart. They will strengthen and Fortify you to stay on course for your life.

- **Jeremiah 31: 31-34,** "Behold, the days come, said the Lord, that I will make a new covenant with the house of Israel and with the house of Judah: not according to the covenant that I made with their fathers in the day that I took them by the hand to bring them out of the land of Egypt: which my covenant they brake, although I was an husband unto them, said the Lord: but this shall be the covenant that I will make with the house of Israel: After those days, said the Lord, I will put my law in their inward parts and write it in their hearts; and will be their God and they shall be my people. And they shall teach no more every man his neighbor and every man his brother, saying, know the Lord: for they shall all know me, from the least of them unto the greatest of them said the Lord: for I will forgive their iniquity and I will remember their sin no more."

- **2 Peter 2:21-22,** "For it had been better for them not to have known the way of righteousness, than after they have known it, to turn from the holy commandment delivered unto them. However, it is happened unto them according to the true proverb, the dog is turned to his own vomit again; and the sow that was washed to her wallowing in the mire."

- **Luke 21: 34-36,** "Take heed to yourselves, lest at any time your hearts be overcharged with surfeiting (excessiveness) and drunkenness and care this life and so that day come upon you unawares. For as a snare shall it come on all them that dwell on the face of the whole earth."

**Watch**, therefore, and **Pray Always**, that you may be accounted worthy to escape all things that shall come in our path while in this present world.

- **1 Peter 2:1, 5, 9-11,** "Wherefore laying aside all malice and all guile and hypocrisies and envies and all evil speaking. You also as lively stones are built up a spiritual house, a holy priesthood, to offer up spiritual sacrifices, acceptable to God by Jesus Christ. But you are a chosen generation, a royal priesthood, an holy nation, a peculiar people, that you should show forth the praises of Him who has called you out of darkness into his marvelous light. Which in time past were not a people, but are now the people of God: which had not obtained mercy, but now have obtained mercy. Dearly beloved, I beseech you as strangers and pilgrims, abstain from fleshly lusts, which war against the soul; having your conversation honest among the Gentiles; that where as they speak against you as evil doers, they may by your good works, which they shall behold, glorify God in the day of visitation."

We must understand that submission to the Word of God in love and yielding to the Word of God is a key in the building, equipping and fortifying in your Spiritual walk to be Victorious.

Jesus Christ left the Holy Spirit to teach, his anointing cleanses our life and sends you in the direction of the Gospel to assist in saving souls.

In other words, when you allow the Spirit of God, which is the breath of life that was breathe into your nostrils, speak to your heart, it will send you in a direction that cleanses. The Word of God starts working in your heart and the energy flows to your mind. The Holy Spirit will have you examine motives before you make a move in any direction of your life.

In the new direction, Faith must be the substance of things you hoped for, and faith that believes in God's Word is complete confidence and trust in everything hoped for and desired, accompanied by expectation and anticipation according to the scripture.

**KEY:** Substance is what is written or said in the Word of God.

**WHAT A GOD FILLED AND GLORIOUS DAY!!!!**

**THINK ON THESE QUESTIONS BELOW:**

1. Do we exist as a people?

2. Do the words exist on the pages in the Bible?

3. Do you have faith that believes and trust in the words in the Bible?

4. Do you words exitst on the pages of an author you know that gives good advice a book?

5. Is it unbelievable to trust what is written by the people who were inspired by God?

6. Do you believe these people were and are inspired by GOD?

Let us walk by Faith, not by sight, Believe and Trust in the Words written in the Bible, it will heal all manner of disease, set the captive free, loose chains that hold, undo heavy burdens, miracles will happen right before your eyes.

The people of the world enjoys doing things in a manner without the principles in the Word of God. They feel restricted when applying the Word of God to their life. The people of the world like a loose life, where anything goes. Therefore, we must walk by the Word of God, not by what we see in the natural. We call those things that are not as though they were. The just shall live by faith, and by faith we are counted as righteous. It's better to obey God's Word by faith, than to sacrifice what you feel is right to please man or fleshly desires.
**Listen and Obey the Word of God**

**Who is our Authority? God**

**What is our Authority? God's Words**

**Revelation 22:12-17** tells us, "Behold, I come quickly; and my reward is with me, to give every man according as his work shall be. I am Alpha and Omega, the beginning and the end, the first and the last. Blessed are they that do his commandments that they may have a right to the tree of life and may enter in through the gates into the city. For without are dogs and sorcerers and whoremongers and murderers and idolaters and whosoever loves and makes a lie. I, Jesus, have sent mine angel to testify unto you these things in the churches. I am the root and the offspring of David and the bright and morning star. I am the way, the truth and the light. Put on the strength that is in Christ Jesus our Lord and Savior. Therefore being justified by faith, we have peace with God through our Lord Jesus Christ. For when we were yet without strength, in due time Christ died for the ungodly."

**Proverbs 14:25-27** tells us, "A true witness delivers souls, but a deceitful witness speaks lies. In the fear of the Lord is strong confidence: and his children shall have a place of refuge. The fear of the Lord is a fountain of life, to depart from the snares of death. Again I say, put on the strength in Christ Jesus." The strength comes from your belief in, and you being a doer of, the Word of God.

**Proverbs 24:1-5** tells us, "Be not thou envious against evil men, neither desire to be with them. For their hearts study destruction and their lips talk of mischief. Through wisdom is a house built; and by understanding it is established: and by knowledge shall the chambers be filled with all precious and pleasant riches. A wise man is strong; yea, a man of knowledge increaseth strength."

**Proverbs 10:29** tell us, "The way of the Lord is strength to the upright: but destruction shall be to the workers of iniquity."

**Whosoever will, let him come freely to drink of the cup.**

**Those that hunger and thirst after righteousness shall be filled.**

**Ephesians 6:11-20** tells us, "Put on the whole armor of God, that you may be able to stand against the wiles of the devil. For we wrestle not against flesh and blood, but against principalities, against powers, against the rulers of the darkness of this world, against spiritual wickedness in high places. Wherefore take unto you the whole armor of God, that you may be able to withstand in the evil day and having on the breastplate of righteousness: and your feet shod with the preparation of the gospel of peace; above all, taking the shield of faith, wherewith you shall be able to quench all the fiery darts of the wicked. And take the helmet of salvation and the sword of the Spirit, which is the Word of God;

praying always with all prayer and supplication in the Spirit; and watching thereunto with all perseverance and supplication for all saints: and for me, that utterance may be given unto me, that I may open my mouth boldly, to make known the mystery of the gospel, for which I am an ambassador in bonds: that there in I may speak boldly, as I ought to speak."

**James 1:2-8** tells us, "My brother, count it all joy when you fall into diverse (various) temptations; knowing this, that the trying of your faith works patience. Nevertheless, let patience have her perfect work, that you may be perfect and entire, wanting nothing. If any of you lack wisdom, let him ask of God, that gives to all men liberally and upbraideth not; and it shall be given him. But let him ask in faith, nothing wavering. For he that wavers is like a wave of the sea driven with the wind and tossed. For let not that man think that he shall receive anything of the Lord. A double-minded man is unstable in all his ways. **"Who can trust him?"**

**James 1:12-17** tells us, "Blessed is the man that endures temptation: for when he is tried, he shall receive the crown of life, which the Lord hath promised to them that love Him. Let no man say when he is tempted, I am tempted of God: for God cannot be tempted with evil, neither tempteth he any man: But every man is tempted, when he is drawn away of his own lust and enticed. Then when lust hath conceived, it bringeth forth sin: and sin, when it is finished, bringeth forth death. Do not err, my beloved brother. Every good gift and every perfect gift is from above and cometh down from the Father of lights with whom are no variables (changeability or fickleness), neither shadow of turning.

**KEY:** Put into action the gifts you receive from God in a righteous way and your pathway will be clear.

Let us be reminded of the words of **James 1:22-25**, "Be you doers of the Word and not hearers only, deceiving your own selves. For if any be a hearer of the Word and not a doer, he is like unto a man beholding his natural face in a glass: For he beholds himself and goes his way and straightway forgets what manner of man he was. But who so, look into the perfect law of liberty and continues therein, he being not a forgetful hearer, but a doer of the Word, this man shall be blessed in his deed."

Let us put on the strength that is in Christ Jesus and walk circumspectly, to go and do spiritual battle.

## CHAPTER 7

## NOW YOU CAN BATTLE IN THE MOST HOLY FAITH

## BATTLE IN THE MOST HOLY FAITH

### We have been through the process of:

- Building in the most holy faith (having faith-that-believes in Jesus Christ)

- Equipping in the most holy faith (putting on the whole armor of God to assist in standing firm in God's Holy Word by faith)

- Fortifying in the most holy faith (wearing the Strength of Jesus Christ by faith).

I pray the Holy Spirit has enlightened your understanding of the heart, to break chains that form strongholds, that bind and demonic bands that keep you from having Victory in your Spiritual Walk.

In the battle, understand, you must be patient to see what the spirit of the Lord has to reveal to you. Have confidence in the Word of God. Resist Satan's wicked devices and never operate from a position of greed, which says, "I need it," or pride, which says, "I deserve it."

It is critical to get an understanding: This is a spiritual battle. God will fight the battle if you will be still. This is not up for debate! Understand God is all He says He is. Just speak the Word of God in love out of a pure heart and be patient. We wrestle not against flesh and blood, but against principalities, against powers, against the rulers of darkness of this world, against spiritual wickedness in **high places**.

When God speaks, "Be still, and know that I am God," he is speaking to your free will.

Let us think about the story in Mark 1:23-27, Jesus spoke to the spirits inside the wild man. This man was truly tired of being tormented by those spirits, but he could not free himself. The Word of God had to be spoken directly to the spirits that had him bound. The enemy continued to torment him in his mind, until he came into the presence of Jesus who spoke directly to those spirits that were tormenting him. The man was loosed from those spirits by the authority of the Word of

God.

Be still in your free will and know that God's Word will prevail over the power of darkness.

The enemy works with the power of divination to control the mind of man, so that he can suggest selfish thoughts that keep you in bondage to the flesh. The power of divination is a strong force the enemy is applying to possess the Body of Christ. It's a spirit that holds you in sin and slowly sucks the life out of you, until you are spiritually dead or have no desire for change for the good of yourself or all man-kind, not understanding your wayward lifestyle can and will affect you and others.

**KEY:** "Submit yourselves therefore to God. Resist the
devil and he will flee from you."

When walking in the status of the Word of God, you have power to tread over scorpions and over all the power of the enemy and nothing shall by any means hurt you.

Never quit or give up when in the fight. Those who keep persevering will finish the race victoriously in Christ Jesus.

Paul said, "I press toward the mark for the prize of the high calling in Christ Jesus." Paul is reaching toward something, he understands is best for him and others. As the enemies see you reaching higher in Christ Jesus, he will make every effort to put in action whatever and whomever he can to deter your progress in a righteous manner. However, understand, satan wants you to loose heart, his goal are to steal the seed, which is the Word of God that has been planted in your life, so you will revert to a sinful nature.

Press upward in the Word of God from heart the with all that is within you. Keep your heart and face set like flint, understanding God does everything except fail in what HE wants to accomplish in our life and in this present world. What may look like failure to you, is an opportunity for God to show His hand strong and mighty concerning the matters in our life.

Remember that the enemy can never stop you, perhaps delay God's plan for our life. If delayed, there is something within you that is not ready to receive what God has for you. God knows what is best although weary eyes can not see, just say Thank

You Lord, and do not complain.

God allows you to go through the refining and purifying in our lives to be like gold, and how deep-rooted the sin is, will determine how intense the battle will be.

In all you do and say, while in the heat of the battle, keep this in the heart:

**Love conquers all.**
**Love never fails.**
**Love covers all sin.**

**Testimony:** I would like be transparent with all my readers. I first came back to the Word of God, sincerely in need of a better way of life. I cried for help and Jesus answered. Seventeen years ago, my intent when I returned to the Word of God, was to study God's Word to be morally clean. I learned at a young age the Word of God has good clean principles, and standards for life. Since I rededicated my life seventeen years ago, the Holy Spirit has taken me higher in Him day by day. The journey is great! I honestly love it! I would not turn back for anything in this present world. It is richer than what the world's standards can offer. OH! Taste the Lord thy God, he is sweeter than the honey in the honeycomb. I understand just as a pattern of a tree is in a small acorn, so is the pattern of my life in the seed drop in my mothers womb.

**KEY:** Place your hand on the Gospel (**Word of God**), if any man should look back he is not worthy for the kingdom of heaven.

**Look back: a desire for what you left in this present world**

God is love. Love covers all sins. If I am a child of the King, I must love all men unconditionally out of a pure heart in spirit and truth. God knows our hearts, even our thoughts afar off. So, love your enemies, they are truly a blessing in disguise.

God said, he would make your enemy your footstool. He will prepare a table in the presence of your enemy. God is saying to us that he will use them to elevate you, if you abide by his principles in love.

**KEY:** If you abide in God's principles in love in spirit
and truth, that bad situation the enemy created
is the step to go higher in life. God is speaking to
you right here: "Do not get weary in well doing,
for in due season you shall reap a harvest if
faint not."

It is all up to you. Stay steadfast, unmovable, always abounding
in the work of the Lord, for as much as you know that your labor
is not in vain in the Lord. The enemy knows it and he is there to
trick or deceive you to do his will. If you do not allow God's Word
to come into your heart to remove the sin in your life, you will
continue to walk in the way of darkness and be blind in that
place of your life.

You can only apply what you understand to be true in the Word
of God. Action comes by faith-that-believes and trusts according
to the scriptures.

You know now that faith without works is dead. James 2:17-26
tells us, "Even so, faith, if it has not works, is dead, being alone.
A man may say, thou have faith and I have works: show me thy
faith without thy works and I will show thee my faith by my
works. Thou believe that there is one God; thou do well: the
devils also believe and tremble. However, will thou know, o vain
man, that faith without works is dead? Was not Abraham our
father justified by works, when he had offered Isaac his
son upon the altar? See thou how faith formed with his
works and by works was faith made perfect?

In addition, the scripture was fulfilled which said,
"Abraham believed God and it was imputed unto him for
righteousness: and he was called the friend of God. You
see by works a man is justified and not by faith only.
Faith by works justified Rehab the harlot, when she had
received the messengers and had sent them out another way? For
as the body without the spirit is dead, so faith without works is
dead also."

**KEY:** The Holy Spirit has place the Word of God in
our possession to give an understanding of how
to apply it by faith, line by line, precept upon
precept, step by step, day by day to receive his
good promises.

### Love Listens,
#### Love Grows then,
##### Love Flows to Others

Now you must do a spiritual checkup and remove any obstacle that can be a stumbling block, which keeps you from running this race at a steadfast pace by Faith-that-Believes and Trust. You shall speak to theMountain, remove from this place to a distance place and it shall be move; and nothing shall be impossible unto you.

It is the steadfastness of the Word of God applied in true love that cuts, going and coming, dividing the true from the false to know the intent of the heart. Without love, the sword is dull and of no effect, which indicate you are not applying the Word of God in Love to Heal, Mend, Undo, and Bind. Whenever the Word of God is applied without Love it is of no effect, you will get frustrated and begin to operate out of flesh desires in accordance to the world's standards.

God said, His ways are not ours, His thoughts are higher, as far as the Heaven is high above the earth, so great is his mercy towards them that fear Him.

Have patience in love; remember that to fear the Lord is the beginning of knowledge.

### KEY: LOOSE YOUR HOPE IN THE WORD OF GOD!

Now let us understand, there are two critical hindrances that keeps you from victory in your spiritual walk: faith that believes and trust not and our out spoken tongue in an ungodly manner.

Pray at this time: "Search me, dear Lord, if there is anything in me that doesn't represent you, take it out and strengthen me with your Holy Word."

Know that the enemy wants to destroy what God has purposed for your life. Satan will attack you emotionally, physically, financially, and spiritually. Satan's greatest tool is your past. He loves to operate from your past wrong doings of your life.

Let us be truly cleansed of our past life with the Word of God, in which in times past we operated from our free will, that did not exemplify the Word of God. This means, do not have an unfinished past, before moving to the next place in your life, are you could find yourself in a place where you will begin to slip back in your old nature, and begin to question was I truly delivered through the Word of God, or did I just go through the motions to appear as though the Word of God saved me.

The biggest blunder people make in their life spiritually, is to receive a false sense of victory from satan. Knowing they did not complete their past problems by staying committed to the Word of God in spirit and truth in order to be grounded in the Word of God, so they will not be moved, before moving to the next place in your life.

Now, let us look at sin. Sin is what the serpent (non-believers) says is the **IN** thing. The same serpent that beguiled Eve, speaks to the people in the world today in the same manner to make you question God's will and way for your life. Do not take the bait. We know that once sin takes root, if not immediately addressed from the heart with the Word of God, it will grow. Moreover, because sin feels good to the body, it is hard to free it from the body, because it has taken root in the soul of man. You will acquire the taste for the sin and the spirit will not be strong enough to overcome because you have not built, equipped, fortified the spirit with the Word of God to be an overcomer in that area of your life.

Do not be foolish and take the bait as Eve did, and then try to blame it on someone else. This is a spirit from satan, you are accussing someone else for your sin or sins and who is satan? **An accusser of the brethren.**

Take ownership of your wrongs. Do not play the blame game, as though it is someone else fault because you took the bait. Apply the Word of God to that situation and the Word of God will go to work cleansing you inside out to be clothe in the righteousness of God. As far as the East is from the West, so will your sin be forgiven and remembered no more by God. The only reason you will remember your sin or sins, is in being thankful and grateful from the horrible pit God brought you out of, knowing God set your feet on a solid rock and has established your goings Victoriously in Christ Jesus.

**TWO WRONGS NEVER MAKE IT RIGHT**

"Vengeance belongs to God. Do not render evil for evil unto any man; but forever follow that which is good, both among you and to all men. Rejoice evermore and pray without ceasing." **1 Thessalonians 5:15-17**, for this is the will of God in Christ Jesus, concerning your life.

**KEY: How can sin have you bound, unless it first binds the strong man? Is your spirit man strong?**

Sometimes we are asked to wait upon the Lord. God is never late. So, wait quietly and put your hope in his Holy Word. When God's Word goes forth, it will not return void. **Wait I say on Lord, he will not fail you.**

### We must have Faith-that-Believes and Trust:

* Believe that Jesus paid a price for your sins and guilt.
* Believe he redeemed, washed and made you clean.
* Believe that he will satisfy every need created by your history and future.
* Believe and trust that God is a rewarder of them who diligently seek Him.

Have Faith-that-Believes and Trusts that God hears and answer all that call upon his name in spirit and truth.

It will not be what you get in the battle, but what you give in the battle that will determine the worth of life you live. It is better to give than to receive. Love is an important key of what you sow in the battles, to grow out of the battles.

Beauty shines through in the good that you do. Anytime the enemy brings you a lemon, make lemonade. The Word of God is love, it is sweet to the spirit that will conquer the soul, and direct the body in a way of not looking at another person's sins. We have all fallen short of the glory of God. Jesus said that he who is without sin, cast the first stone.

**KEY: IF A BROTHER OR SISTER IS CAUGHT IN SIN; RESTORE HIM GENTLY IN THE WORD OF GOD.**

Represent God's Word in love towards all men, not in hostility or hatred. It is a demonic spirit that makes you think with an attitude of self righteousness, and it brings forth one or all of these attributes: jealousy, revenge, competition, rage, anger, hatred towards men for their indifferent way of life.

Love with your whole heart. Ask Jesus into your heart and He will come in, if you are sincere. When Jesus Spirit enters in, it is like a sweet peace with joy.

Once you call on Jesus, if the enemy can not cause you to sin with the body, he will cause you to sin with your tongue by doing a lot of unhealthy talking. The tongue can do so much good, but it can also cause so much heartbreak and damage to peoples' lives, if we do not speak the principles in the Word of God in spirit and truth.

We must remember that the tongue is a weapon. Be careful how you use it, because of the enormous damage it can and will do. Allow God to be the glory in all we say and do. So we must bridle the tongue.

Read and meditate on the scriptures listed below. They will truly tame the tongue and allow God's Holy Spirit to enter the heart.

- **Psalm 39:1** – "I said, I will take heed to my ways that I sin not with my tongue: I will keep my mouth with a bridle, while the wicked is before me."

- **Proverbs 15:2, 4, 23** – "The tongue of the wise use knowledge aright: but the mouth of fools pour out foolishness. A wholesome tongue is a tree of life: but perverseness therein is a breach in the spirit. A man hath joy by the answer of his mouth: and words spoken in due season how good is it!"

- **Proverbs 18:21** – "Death and life are in the power of the tongue: and they that love it shall eat the fruit thereof."

- **Proverbs 31:26** – "She openeth her mouth with wisdom; and in her tongue is the law of kindness."

- **Matthew 12:34 - 37** – "O generation of vipers, how can you, being evil, speak good things? For out of the abundance of the heart the mouth speaks. Good men out of the good treasure of the heart bring forth good things; and evil men out of the evil treasure bring forth evil things. Nevertheless, I say unto you, that every idle word that men shall speak, they shall give accout thereof in the day of judgement. For by thy [God] words thou shall be justified and by thy [our] words thou shall be condemned."

- **James 3:5-10** – "Even so, the tongue is a little member; and boasteth great things. Behold how great a matter a little fire kindles! And the tongue is a fire, a world of iniquity: so is the tongue among our members, that it defileeth the whole body and sets on fire the course of nature; and it is set on fire of Hell. For every kind of beast and of birds and of serpents and of things in the sea is tamed and hath been tamed of mankind: But the tongue can no man tame: it is an unruly evil, full of deadly poison. Therewith bless we God, even the Father; and therewith curse we men, which are made after the similitude of God. Out of the same mouth proceed blessing and cursing.

  **My brethren, these things <u>ought not so, to be</u>!"**

- **Colossian 4:6** – "Let your speech be always with grace, seasoned with salt, that you may know how you ought to answer every man

**KEY:** Whatever words you speak will create a life or death situation.

### <u>Ask yourself:</u>

1. **Does a fountain send forth at the same place sweet and bitter water?**

2. **Can a fig tree bear olive berries?**

During the battle you can not curse your opponent, then speak God's Word in love, and expect God to hear and answer. Be careful what you speak. Count the cost. Take no offense. Have nothing against your brothers or sisters, but love them and allow God to show you the good in them and focus on that, which is good, and then will they see the light. Do not misunderstand as though God is saying pacify or over look their sin or sins. Gently address the sin or sins, then move on to what is good in their life and build on that.

Understand it's a spirit that is controlling their emotions and decision-making ability in righteousness. So, be patient. Do not worry or frown. It pulls the heart down and shakes the foundation of confidence in faith-that-believes and trusts in doing God's will for your life or concerning others.

We must overcome in our life in order to have spiritual victory. Remember the enemy comes as an angel of light, to draw you in and away from your call and purpose in this present world. Keep in your heart and mind, **"Jesus has called me to holiness and has already established me unto good works"**.

I leave this chapter repeating: in bold letters, **"WATCH AND PRAY,"** because your adversary walks around like a roaring lion seeking whom he can devour. Notice that the word says, **"like** a roaring lion, seeking whom he can devour."** We know that Satan needs a vessel to work in and through to bring harm to you. Let us not forget that he will work in and through our emotions and decision-making ability to do harm to the welfare of our brethren.

### Do Not Take the Bait!!

**Will you allow Satan's spirit to use you?**

**Will you allow Satan and his foes to devour you?**

## KEY:  Manners will matter in the battle; Love is not rude!

Before the we go any further I must enlighten you regarding the spirit that is lurking in our churches today.

Satan has a special interest in the Body of Christ. We can well-believe, he will do everything in his power to sidetrack, hinder, weaken, and destroy the ministry of the Church. The devil's organizational set-up calls for a demon prince to be assigned to each local expression of the church.

Many churches have a history of certain types of problems. The spirit prince over that church can readily be identified by the church's specific type of problem.

For instance, in some churches you will find a spirit of strife... members striving with members. Strife is one of Satan's chief weapons. Satan knows that if he can preoccupy our minds in strife with people, we will not have a desire to pray, read and study the Word of God, to show ourselves approved, a workman that need not be ashamed that can rightly divide the Word of truth, because the struggle with strife of people in our mind has become greater than our prayer and study lifestyle. The more we do not submit to the Word of God, the harder our heart becomes, and the less likely we are willing to respond in a Christ-like manner.

### STRIFE = NO PRAYER LIFE

Another weapon is jealousy and competition that creates a fight to be better than one another. Christians will get puffed up with pride, thinking they are better than others, thinking of themselves more highly than they ought to think. As long as Christians are fighting among themselves for a higher position, they are certainly not fighting against the evil deeds that are running ramport in the Body of Christ. This is one of the reasons why the Church can not go in all the world and conquer souls and this is what Satan wants.

### JEALOUSY AND COMPETITION = NO PRAYER LIFE

Other churches are controlled by false doctrines. For instance, the doctrine may be true, but the devil fosters an obsession with the doctrine. He gets a group so concentrated on one facet of truth (salvation or the Second Coming) that they will neglect to minister the whole counsel of God.

Some churches are still operating from a color concept, thinking each ethnic group should stay with their own race of people. They have satan's spirit of divide to conquer; not truly understanding one race of people do not have all the answers. God created all and Love all man-kind, even those that continue in their sins, but know God do hate the sin that they do.

The root of this spirit that chose to divide, is fear of the unknown, and this fear keeps you separated and brings, bitterness and hatred, selfish, competatiive, deciet, hostility toward the opposite race of people. They pretend when you come into their congregation as though they love, but if you stay with the heart beat of God, you can truly feel inside out, if they have the True

Love of Jesus Christ or are they still holding on to the
generational curse that is in their blood line on the physical side
of their life..

In satan's twisted thoughts and theories, he will have them
justify their attitudes and actions. Satan knows that God is love
and his loves flow from heart to heart. There is no hate in God.
God's Spirit can not flow in and through the people in the
congregation when they are
harboring attributes that are not Christ-like. This
church is operating from a position of free will.

However, through Prayer, they will come to know and
understand, God said, "Whosoever will let him freely
come and drink from the cup." So if this church is truely
ministering the gospel of truth, they will allow all to come freely
to drink from the cup. Why? because they know in their hearts, I
have been chosen by God and given stewardship of his
possessions, I am not the owner, "**SO WHO SO EVER WILL LET
HIM COME**"

### TRADITIONS OF MAN = NO PRAYER LIFE

Some demons are specialists in getting a church to
operate on human talents and abilities rather than upon
the power of the Holy Spirit (having a form of Godliness,
but denying the power thereof.) II Timothy 3:5).

Still today, many people are blinded to the great outpouring of
God's spirit with power , so they continue to operate on man's
power or men with great names, not
looking to the Author and Finisher of their faith.

### NO PRAYER LIFE

Demons of worldliness and materialism rule over some local
churches. They are caught and rapped up in fame and fortune,
rather than souls being delivered and set free from the wages of
sin and death.

### NO PRAYER IN THE CHURCH

There are spirit princes of denominationalism and sectarianism.
Their aim is to keep the body of Christ divided, this is done with
their form of Godliness. Many true followers of Jesus Christ can
see that true spiritual ministry has faded out of sight.

Understand and know, God has his people covered and they will appear in God's timing one by one. These people will be looking for nothing, but the Word of God to be manifested in the church in this earth. These men and women of God will know that freely they received, and freely they give. The ministry will not be about what we are going to get out of it, but what we can give to bring deliverance and freedom in a person's life.

Ask yourself, "Am I seeking the righteousness of Jesus Christ, to be a vessel of honor to assist in building of the Kingdom in the Earth?"

Saturate your mind with the Word of God and hide it in your heart that you might not sin against God. It is not what goes in a man that defiles him, but what come out that defiles a man.

Understand and know, God knows many things will go in a man, because you are in this present world. He also knows, that if you allow it to come out of you, it will begin to take form in your life and become you. This is why God commands us to be doers of the Word of God, so it will take form in our life and become who he created you to be.

**KEY: Keep your heart and thoughts, Pure and Fixed on the Word of God.**

Christian dare not ignore the influence and power of Satan. Do not become preoccupied with it, but stay alert and vigilant, not paralyzed with fear.

Be sure that each day of your life you appropriate the Armor of God in your life, because each piece protects you from the cunning craftiness of Satan and his demonic forces.

Now, let us see each piece of the armor in a more spiritual way and go into a mock battle in our heart and mind as you read the next few pages.

We know that Jesus used each piece of the armor while in battle in the wilderness. He stood against the wiles of the devil. Jesus said that we should do greater works.

John 14:12, "Verily, verily, I say unto you, he that believes on me, the works that I do shall he do also; and greater works than these shall he do; because I go unto my Father."

**BUCKLER OF TRUTH** - is the Word of God as it centers
in your life expediently and appropriated. Truth is
likened to the sword that holds and supports the
sword. Gird up your loins with the truth in God's Word
and reject Satan's lies that comes from free will of
emotions.

The enemy will attack God's Word that is the truth in
Your life, to keep you from having an abundant life. You
will be tested, but understand in your heart the Word of
Truth is what sets you free from Satan's wicked schemes
and devices. If satan gets a grip or foothold in your life,
he does not want to let go. He will try with all the power
that is given to him, to keep you paralyzed with the
thought of: **"I need this" or "I deserve this".**

Then the next time a believer see you, you will be "A double-
minded man unstable in all his ways". Who can trust this
double-minded man? Now you begin to justify the sin that holds
you in your life. Know the truth; Hold onto the truth in your
heart. If truth falls, the Word of God goes and the breastplate of
righteousness will not be fitted properly.

Visualize holding fast to the truth in God's Word in your
heart, for the breastplate of righteousness to fit properly
to walk up rightly before God and recieve favor from God
and Man.

**BREASTPLATE OF RIGHTEOUSNESS** - We wear Christ's own
righteousness formed in you by the Spirit. The breastplate is sure
protection of the heart from satanic attacks. If you take a stand
for something other than what the Word of God speaks expressly
to you. You are standing on human thoughts, which opens the
door to be eventually hit in the heart and fall. Thank God for the
chastisement while you still have a breath of life to take heed,
repent, and turn from wicked ways. If you should not fall in this
life, at the end of your life, you will be hit with the blow of eternal
death.

In the process of putting on Christ robe of righteousness,
understand you have many robes in your life to put on. But only
by being clothed in humility with God's righteousness, can we
walk Victoriously in Christ Jesus through this valley of the
shadow of death, fearing no evil, knowing God is with you.

Be sure your desire for righteousness honors the Word of God. Strive for purity. Understand God did not put defeat in our path, but Victory.

**Roman 8:29-31;** For whom he did foreknow, he also did predestinate to be conformed to the image of his Son, that he might be the firstborn among many brethren. "Moreover whom he did predestinate, these he also called: whom he called, these he also justified: and whom he justified, these he also glorified. What shall we then say to these things? If God be for us who can be against us?"

**KEY: Be an overcomer by the blood of the Lamb and the Words of your testimony.**

The road that leads in the way of Jesus, is narrow, like a tightening on the inside. God is closing in on everything in your life that is not of HIM and setting boundaries around you. It is like you can not move or turn in any direction contrary to the Word of God. What is happening is you are reading God's Word and he is protecting the Good Works he has in stilled in you. The more you are a hearer and doer in the Word of God, the more relaxed and free you feel and the easier it will become to be a doer of the Word of God, and no longer will you feel the tightening on the inside out, but have the posture of liberty and freedom in the Spirit of who God created you to be.

**KEY: THE TIGHTENING IS THE RESTRICTION AWAY FROM A SINFUL NATURE.**

God's righteousness takes you higher in life. You feel free and soar like an eagle with unspeakable joy. Matt. 7:13,14, "Enter you in at the straight gate: for wide is the gate and broad is the way that leads to destruction and many there be which go in thereat: strait is the gate and narrow is the way, which leads unto life and few there be that find it."

**JESUS IS............**

### The Bread of Life
### The Tree of Life
### The Water of Life
### The Fountain of Life
### The Crown of Life

### "He will be the Spirit that gives you Life"

Visualize standing for righteousness in the Word of God,
a lifting will be in your spirit, then you will experience
True Victory over every evil spirit that comes to try you.

**SHOES OF THE GOSPEL** - Shoes are something you wear. The Gospel is the teachings of Jesus, the apostles and the narrative life of Jesus, which is absolute truth. Jesus paralled the Gospels with shoes, for his children to understand this is something you must wear in your life daily. As we know and understand Jesus wore the teachings of the Gospel all the years he was on the earth.

The Gospel prepares us to be good soldiers by giving inner peace to be victorious over Satan and his imps. Did not Jesus say you will tread on the scorpions and nothing shall harm you? In battle, the enemy is put under your feet to be used as a footstool to take you to your next level in life, if you **DO NOT LOSE HEART.**

Carry the Word of God to Jerusalem, Judah, Samaria and the uttermost parts of the world. Spread the Gospel (good news) in spirit and truth. Never take your shoes off. Be prepared in season and out of season. Wherever Jesus traveled, He was alert and ready. He kept his shoes (Word of God) on.

Turn the light switch on in your life; light up the room for people to see Christ Jesus. By keeping your shoes (Word of God) on you are ready to light up the room, with the Gospel of Jesus Christ, wherever the Lord
sends you. The Word is a lamp unto your feet and light
unto your pathway.

Visualize these shoes (Word of God) stepping into a
dark place representing Jesus who is the Light to the

World, sharing the good news with others to make a
difference for the good of mankind in this life and after
life.

**THE SHIELD OF FAITH** - With it you will be able to
quench all the fiery darts of the wicked one. **Ephesians
6:15** reveals satan and his demons have power, but our
God has all authority. Think for a moment: a person can have
power, but if he does not have any authority, the power is of no
effect. The person in authority must give him permission to use
his power.

**Matthew 28:18** reveals, Jesus came and spoke unto them saying
All power is given unto me in heaven and in earth. When
Abraham feared his enemies, God spoke in Genesis 15:1, "Do not
be afraid, Abram. I am your shield, your exceedingly great
reward." David said in Psalms 5:12, "For you, O Lord, will bless
the righteous; with your favor you will surround him as with a
shield." These men of God stood on the Word of God by faith and
it was their shield.

Our God is a shield to give us total protection in our spiritual
warfare. In the battle, do not take the faith out of what you
believe and trust in the Word of God. It is your ability to move
forward in the Word of God. Every time you speak the Word of
God, believing by faith (which is your shield), the fiery darts hit
the sheld and fall to the ground or back to the enemy and have
no effect in your life.

Visualize speaking the Word of God. Your Shield of Faith will
protect and comfort you in spite of false accusations,
discouragement, disappointments, trickery and deceit, death

**HELMET OF SALVATION** – Is for the head. It protects the
thinking process that contains the saving knowledge of Jesus
Christ who came down through 42 generation through a virgin,
innocent with a pure heart and clean hands. Salvation:
redeemed, cleansed, and rescued you from sin and death.

The enemy wants you to take off your helmet of salvation
so he can send negative and doubting thoughts in your
mind concerning your salvation. He knows that the
battle begins in the mind. If he can trick you into doubting,
who you are, whose you are and deceive you into thinking the
way of Jesus Christ is just a scam a lie, or can Jesus Word's
save me, the helmet is slowly lifting from the head, which holds

your thoughts giving the enemy the opportunity to continue to send the doubting people to speak doubt in your life. Remember that many times the devil does things in a subtle, cunning and crafty way, it may not happen all at once.

## "Watch and Pray"

### DO NOT DOUBT - JESUS WORDS SAVES

To assist in keeping the helmet on. Understand in your heart, without a shadow of doubt, that when you speak the Word of God from the heart, Victory shall be yours, if you **DO NOT LOSE HEART IN YOUR SPIRITUAL WALK TO MANIFEST THE WORD OF GOD IN THE NATURAL.**

Stay in the heart beat of God, because timing is the key; he might not come when you want, if you trust him, you will see he places you in the right place at the right time.

Through prayer say yes to God's Will and Way, and NO to your selfish ways, gossiping about others to get people on your side or feel sorry for you, to try and win favor.

### IT IS A TRICK FROM THE ENEMY..
### DO NOT TAKE THE BAIT!!!

This way of life, is not to prove a point to anyone, by trying to make things happen quickly, by using people? God only acts quickly in an emergency or urgent situation. Think about what makes you react quickly to assist a person. You serve a Sovereign God who knows what's best. **Keep the helmet of Salvation on your head** and trust in God's Word.

Visualize keeping the helmet on your head, so words of An untamed tongue can not reach the mind to affect your heart.

Know and understand, the helmet is the saving knowledge of Jesus Christ that holds your thoughts, to protect the heart and it causes the words of an untamed tongue to be confronted by the Spirit of God that is living and abiding within your soul. It is the same as if your big brother went to fight for you and said stand behind me I got this fight in the Name of Jesus.

Let us meditate on the story; of David and Goliath, when David went to the battlefield to fight for God's people. David ask, Who is this man speaking this way to the army of the Living God. Why doesn't someone go out and kill him? While all the men were being fearful, David thought of a plan. He said, if no one else will go, then I shall fight this enemy of God's people. David said, I have fought with lions and bears when they tried to steal my sheep. I am not afraid to fight this Philistine. God saved me from the Lion's jaw and the paw's of the bear and I trust he will save me from this enemy that I shall fight for God and his people. Goliath laughed at what David brought to the battle, but David said to Goliath **"YOU COME AGAINST ME WITH A SWORD, A SPEAR AND A DART, BUT I COME IN THE NAME OF THE LORD OF HOSTS, THE GOD OF THE ARMIES OF ISRAEL. THIS DAY THE LORD WILL GIVE YOU INTO MY HANDS"**.

KEY:  IN DAVID'S HEART HE WENT TO THE BATTLE
      HAVING AN ASSURANCE,THAT GOD HAS
      GIVEN ME EVERYTHING NEEDED TO HAVE
      VICTORY OVER THIS ENEMY

**THE SWORD OF THE SPIRIT** – Is the Word of God. Be sure the words you speak are seasoned with salt **(Hebrew 4:15)**.

When you lift your sword, lift it in love and truth. God said to bind love and truth around our neck not only will we have favor with him, but he will also give us favor with man.

When Jesus was led by the Spirit into the wilderness to have personal combat with Satan, he was tempted (tested) in every point that we are, yet without sin.

The all-powerful sword, which is the Word of God, was given to Joshua and the Israelites in **Deuteronomy 4:4-6**, "But you that did cleave unto the Lord your God are alive every one of you this day. Behold, I taught you statutes and judgments, even as the Lord my God commanded me, that you should do so, in the land whither you go to posses it. Keep therefore and do them; for this is your wisdom and your understanding in the sight of the nations, which shall hear all these statutes and say, surely this great nation is a wise and understanding people.

**In Matthew 4:4**, Jesus said, "It is written. Man shall not live by bread alone, but by every word that proceeds out of the mouth of

God."

Jesus used the inerrant (free from error) Word of God as the offensive (position of attacking) weapon and defeated Satan. Jesus defense was God himself.

We must do likewise. The sword is the best way to ward off satanic thrusts. It cuts going and coming, to divide the true from false, to show the intent of the heart.

Visualize going into action in love with the sword of the Spirit (Word of God). Each time you act on the Word of God in love, you are warding off the satanic thrusts from the enemy, if you have faith-that-believes and trusts.

**PRAYER** – Pray always with all prayer and supplication with thanksgiving in the Spirit. Unceasing prayer must always go ahead of you before you engage in spiritual battle. Without prayer, you have no power and no clear direction in righteousness and no protection.

Prayer is the appropriation of all the believer's resources in Christ.

Prayer is the strength in Christ Jesus that gives you the ability to walk and stand when everything else is falling apart.

**What you pray in secret,
God will reward you openly!**

Visualize praying and receiving wisdom, instructions with understanding, direction and correction, that gives knowledge, love, peace and joy, which gives you a passion and ability to take action in God's Holy Word.

My prayer and hope is in reading and meditating on the Words of God along with my experiences I have shared in this book, you have become strong in the Lord, and in the power of God's might, prepared with God's ability to defeat territorial spirits in your life.

The spirits that come to kill, steal, and destroy your spirit, soul, and body is in the thoughts of your mind. Yes these spirits that come to kill, steal and destroy is in a physical body, but if you speak and walk in the spirit of the Word of God, that serpent will surely die.

After you have done all in love according to the Word of God, stand knowing God will protect and deliver you from all hurt, harm and danger in your spirit, soul, and body.

**KEY:   God will never leave you nor forsake you**

God's kingdom is coming in this earth. "Thy kingdom come thy will be done in the earth, as it is in Heaven." In other words, what is happening in Heaven, God will cause it to happen in the earth, if we pray without ceasing, **God's Will, will be done?**

Speak truth from the heart and do not be deceived by thoughts in your mind, will and emotions, that is contrary to the Word of God, pretending as though you are being obedient to the Word of God. **"By God's Word, thou shall be justified and by your own words, thou shall be condemned".**

**Are you Built, Equipped, and Fortified to Walk in Spiritual Victory?**

**Are you a willing vessel to bring Heavens to earth?**

May God Bless each one of you who have contributed to the Kingdom of God. May God strengthen your heart to stand on his Promises in his Word, to be able to stand against the wiles of the devil in this present world?

Have faith-that-believes and trusts from the heart, to be more than a conqueror, mighty through the Word of God, which gives you the ability to bring every thought into captivity and pull down strongholds that come against the knowledge of God's Word that is with you.

Understand in your heart, God called you and he will protect you. In addition, he will hold your hand.

**"Victory is yours," says the Lord,
If you do not Lose Heart.**

Be Blessed and Assured and keep your hands to the Gospel plow, not looking back, for if you look back you are not worthy of the Kingdom of Heaven.

Be Blessed and Assured that Jesus is with you even to the ends of this present world.

The next few pages will bring you to a state of mind where you will become fully persuaded of the way to go in Jesus Christ; morally, economically, socially, physically, mentally and most of all spiritually.

God is Spirit and you are spirit, soul and body, but many chose to operate from their free-will in the soulish realm which is close to thier body, which carries a sinful appetite.

**Now let us move forward in the Spirit of Truth of God to conclude this inspired book:**

**CHAPTER 8**

**CONTINUE TO ENTER IN
THE HOUSE OF GOD**

**CONCLUSION**

## CONCLUSION

The Spirit of God that has inspired me to write this book will close the entire book by concluding with this:

We have walked through wisdom, which we know is the principle thing to possess before we can walk in Faith and Love, with an understanding.

We have walked in Faith and Love to come to an understanding, without faith-that-believes and trusts we can not speak to the mountains in life and have them removed. In addition, without faith, it is impossible to please God. We learned we must have unconditional love, because without Love the Word of God is of no effect.

We learned three truths that keeps you in a posture that operates by the principles in the Word of God.
**(SEEK, SPEAK AND LIVE TRUTH)**

We now learned of ten principles given to me by the power of the Holy Spirit to have the ability to Walk in Spiritual Victory.

We know to never cease in praying.

Morning and evening prayer are the best form of meditation. You are communicating in spirit that will give internal exercise and healing to the heart which sends energy to the mind, enabling the body to go in the direction the true you that day and for your life.

Prayer is to obtain complete oneness with the spirit. The oneness brings peace, joy, love and harmony in one's self and gives the ability to share these attributes with others.

The Bible mentions spirit, soul, and body. Let us review them in part so we can define how to operate according to the Word of God, because we know the Word is spirit.

**The Spirit of God has three parts:**
1) **conscience**
2) **intuition**
3) **communication**

God breathed a breath of life into man and man became a living soul. God is a Spirit and those that worship Him shall worship him in spirit and truth. Understand the breath of life is God himself, which became a living soul. The body was formed from the dust of the ground.

Let us stop to remember although God gave us life, He also gave us a free will. You must decide whom you will serve God or man, in other words will you serve Spirit or Flesh, and whom you serve, is whom you will follow.

Jesus says, "Be ye Holy, for I am Holy." You are royal priesthood, a holy nation. You are ambassadors, representatives for Jesus Christ. This lets us know we must operate from spirit, because that is where God is.

The five earthly senses help you know right from wrong, but this is knowledge from our conscience.

The direct knowledge and feelings that are <u>not</u> limited to space or time is the intuition and when it is processed properly, it is direct contact with God himself. He will only speak through His Word, and we know the letter of the law killeth, but the Spirit of God gives life.

Understand mankind has been given a free will, but God is spirit. We all have his spirit living and abiding in our soul. However, many have muffled the voice of God's spirit and have chosen their free-will, which is knowledge and experiences from the the worlds standards, without the Word of God.

Children of God, Friends and Servants of Jesus, understand education is an excellent method to obtain knowledge, but educational knowledge without the application of the Word of God leads your life on dead roads. You may or will recieve good in the land while living from this stand point, but when you leave this earth what shall go with you **"ONLY THE WORKS BY FAITH YOU HAVE DONE ACCORDING TO THE WORD OF GOD"** it is **ESSENTIAL** that you seek the things of God and his righteousness.

Not everyone chooses to govern their life according to the Word of God, therefore it is critical to your spirit **not** to allow anyone to counsel or give you advise in the direction you should go, unless they are Spiritually grounded in the Word of God or you have observed a person baring good fruits in their life that is in line with the Word of God, because we do have good people in this world that do not follow the Word of God, but their deeds are in line with the Word of God. You never know who the Spirit of God will use to get you on the path of the true you.

The truth is you need **not** seek outside for answers. The truth is, God has placed the answers you need in your spirit, but sometimes we muffle the sweet voice of God Spirit speaking to our heart, and listen to others who is not conformed in Holiness.

God will send a vessel with his Words down our path for corrections, instructions in righteousness, to encourage, rebuke to have fellowship, in hope that you grab hold to God's Word that are being spoken to move you in HIS direction for your life.

This direction will slowly awaken your spirit and confirm what was spoken to your heart one step at a time. Please do not rush it. God knows when you can leap, and not become weary, walk and not faint, In Jesus Name, and May God Be Edified and Glorified. **IN AND THROUGH YOUR LIFE.**

**Let us look at the soul, it has three parts: 1) emotions 2) thoughts 3) decision-making ability or will power.**

We know emotions is a reaction toward something or someone.

The ideas and opinions that are limited to space and time are peoples' thoughts, not God's Word.

Decision-making ability (or will power) is a person's ability to determine or make a judgment. Ideas and opinions without God's wisdom are fruitless. Nevertheless, ideas and opinions in conjunction with God's wisdom and principles will make our lives fruitful. This is why we govern our life according to the Word of God and understand God's Words is a Faith Walk, not by what we see, but what we hear according to the Word of God.

**KEY:  The Word of God does not change,
        It is Yes and Amen.**

**NEVERTHELESS, HIS METHODS WILL CHANGE!**

**Roman 6:6, 7** says that our old man is crucified with Him, that
the body of sin might be destroyed, that henceforth we should
**not serve sin**. For he that is dead is **freed from sin**.

### Ask yourself, "Have I died to my free will?"

The spirit has a <u>mind</u> that recieve directions from the heart, while
the soul has a <u>mind</u> that receive directions from either God's Will
or Free will **(The Soul has a choice, but the Spirit can only
move on God's commands).** The free will operate out of
emotions, trigger thoughts and decision-making ability without
the Word of God and is subject to change at any time.

The mind of the soul must be in subjection to the mind of the
spirit of God for it to hear and do what the Spirit of God is
expressingly speaking to the heart.

God said, a double-<u>minded</u> man is unstable in all his ways. This
is the soul of a man that is not recieving a Word from the Spirit of
God, so it switches back and forth in his decision making ability,
looking for ways to please the lust of the flesh, or protect their
pride in life.

**WHO CAN TRUST A MAN WITH A DOUBLE MIND?**

Space and time limits the body. Space and time has a
beginning and end. King Solomon said, "A time to be
born and a time to die." This lets us know that the body
is in a limited space. This body was formed from the
dust of the ground that is in the earth, and it shall return to the
dust of the ground in this earth.

The Holy Spirit is our guide and gives direction only
through the Word of God. Understand the Word of God
is not limited to space and time. If passion is in our
heart for God's way of life, we will take action according
to the Word of God, and we will not be limited to or by
what we see, feel, hear or taste.

The soul of man holds emotions, thoughts, and decision-making ability, which are limited by space and time. If you operate according to the soul, without the spirit of God, you will be bound to what you see, feel, hear, and taste.

The soul of this body performs the eating, sex, fighting, entertainment, and ungodly manners. The body was formed from the dust of the ground, so the body is a dummy that does not know what to do until it gets a signal from the spirit of God, or the soul without the spirit of God.

If you have not Built, Equipped, and Fortified in the Word of God the spirit will not be strong enough to send the signal to the soul, because the soul has muffle the voice of the Spirit of God, which means the body will operate from the soul without the Spirit of God, which holds all your emotions, thoughts, decision-making abilities and will be subject to do or say whatever makes the body feel satisfied, because it has not been strengthen in the Word of God.

In this life we are faced with many obstacles and challenges, that we must over come. But we can only overcome the obstacles and challenges by the Word of God.

In this life we are faced with, rebellion, gluttoning, (eating disorders), divorces, adulteress, pride, deception, murder, sexual immorality, greed, (wanting more money to satisfy a thirst that cannot be satisfied), coveting, fame.

Do not place emphasis on the way the world governs their lives, understand God has given them free will and they have a right to exercise it in this life. So pray for their soul to be set free from the sins that have them bound in this life, because this we know God Love all he have created, but he hates the sin they do. God called you to Holiness and ordered your steps down their path, for you to Pray and be an example in and through the Word of God in spirit and truth.

At **NO COST** should you neglect to strengthen the heart of who you are truly created to be (i.e., a spirit-man). Study the Word of God, show you approve, a work man that needs not to be ashamed, rightly divides the words in spirit and truth. Being an example to the people in this world.

Ever since the spiritual fall of Adam and Eve, the mind of the soul without the Spirit of God have ruled the body. Therefore, the spirit is weak and unaware, muffled by a soul that has become the master, without the Spirit of God. We know the body is a dummy that recieves from the soul and without the spirit all the body wants and know, what makes me feel good. The body has no sense of principles, standards, moral, or directions. It has to receive a signal fromthe heart of the spirit or the mind of the soul in order for it to go in any given direction.

The soul is an interface and it directs the emotions, thoughts and decision-making ability to fulfill the needs of the body. When you operate from the soul without God's Spirit, you are limited to space and time. This is why people take matters into their own hands. They see no way out of the space and time in which they live because they are operating out of the soul without the Spirit of God. **(they are operating out of free will)** If the Spirit of God does not inspire the soul, it will take what God meant for the good and turn it around for evil. As we learned earlier in the book turn evil around and it spells **"LIVE."**

### DO YOU WANT TO LIVE AN ABUNDANT LIFE?

Let us look at this: the soul without the Spirit of God will take love and turn it into lust, take a fight and turn it into weapons, warfare, strategies, bombs, etc.

Satan, sits in the seat of your soul without the Spirit of God and will begin to deceive you into justifying your wrongs with believing the twisted theories and ideas he has placed in your mind in order to do his will in the earth.

### PLEASE UNDERSTAND, GOD WILL HAVE THE FINAL SAY IN THIS EARTH, AMEN

Let me enlighten you: God has given unto you eternal life, not eternal death, but when you **do not** consult the Word of God (which is the spirit that was given to you when God breathe a breath of life into your nostrils and you became a living soul), then your desire is to do your will and where your will is these are the deeds you will do and your deeds sends you in a direction of your destiny. Understand tese deeds will seem good, but when you hold them up in the light of the Word of God you can see the imperfection in your desire which is willing you to do these deeds that will wage an eternal death for your soul.

**KEY:** Do not play the blame game, you are in control of your body, moreover, the final answer or move

you make is up to you, and blame others is saying
you are not in control of your decisions that is
being executed from the body you live in.

Understand the body does not know what is good for it, it waits
to receive a transmitting signal from the spirit or soul. When the
message is relayed from the Spirit of God to the soul and then to
the body, the body becomes disciplined to do the Word of God.
You are now following the divine will of God for your life. It fills
you with love, peace, and joy in the Holy Spirit. By governing
your life in this manner, you are being shaped in the likeness
and image our Jesus Christ. You are a Son of God, an
overcomer and shall have many Victories in your life, if
you **do not lose heart** in your Spiritual Walk. You are
spiritualizing your body to operate in the manner God ordained it
to be in this life and the afterlife.  You ar part of bringing
Kingdom Living, as it is in Heaven, it will be in the earth.

I cannot express this enough. Have faith-that-believes
and trusts in the Word of God that is speaking to
your heart, that sends you in the direction God's has
predestined for your life, before the foundation of the world and
before you stepped in time. " I am the Lord thy God that teach
you to profit and lead you in the way you shall go."

Be as close to perfection as God has given you the ability
to be. God knows your imperfections that will cause you
to fall short of the Glory.

My prayer is that you can gather everything the Holy Spirit has
given me to share with you, so you can walk in the same or even
greater Victories that I have seen and experienced, since I gave
my life back to Jesus Christ seventeen years ago.

### TO GOD BE THE GLORY!!

Know that through our persistence we receive success, but
success comes only from following the essentials, which we know
is in the Word of God.

If you are open to change through the Word of God, what seemed
destined to be a failure in your life will be assured survival?

Never get bitter at the failures in your life, because it will cause
you to miss the excellent opportunity to become a better person
in this life and the afterlife.

You need knowledge, with God's wisdom and understanding to make decisions in this life, in order to have the confidence to walk in the parameters or boundaries that has been set for you before the foundation of the world and before you stepped into time.

I know many people see abiding in God's Word as a risk, to their position, relationships, socialize events, work place, and with some people in the churches that do not follow God's principles and standards for their life in spirit and truth. Understand these people will not be there with you to answer for you at the end of your life. The God of Heaven will only want to know, "What did you do with the commands Jesus left for you to do," So we must make a choice, and say to ourselve, "No matter what come or go" for God's Word will I live by, and for God's Word will I die in, even if I must walk alone in this physical world I live in. Jesus did say, we might have to forsake, mother, father, sister, brother, daughters, sons, etc when following his ways.

**KEY: To have Victory without doing the Word of God in Spirit and Truth is to triumph without God's Glory.**

As the Spirit of God ends this book: Understand God is Our Father which art in Heaven, and no one will share His Glory. God is All Knowing, All Powerful, and All Present at all times. He will never leave you nor forsake you. God's Word will see you through your valley of the shadow of death, so fear no evil, for God is with you.

**THE WORD OF GOD IS THE LIGHT THAT SHINES BRIGHT IN THE VALLEY, FOR YOU TO SEE IT IS JUST A SHADOW.**

Go with Believing Faith that trusts with Confidence in the direction of your dream. Go live a worthy life in Christ Jesus in this present world. Be instant in season and out of season; reprove, rebuke, exhort in order to enhance the quality of each day of your life in Christ Jesus.

God commanded us to preach the Gospel. Be doers of the Word of God, not a hearer only. It is better to not know the Word of God, than to know the Word of God and do it not, to him is sin. Hide the Word of God in your Heart, hold integrity true in your hearts even if no one is watching, because this I know, God sees all, knows all and even knows our thoughts afar off.

May God grant you the faith-that-believes and trust with strength to face adversities in this life. Faith-that-believes and trust with strength is resistance to fear? You must respect and honor man, but not fear man, for man can only destroy the physical being of who you think makes you as a person, but it is the spirit of God that makes you a beautiful butterfly.

The Word of God teaches you the mastery of fear, but not the absence of fear. Why the Word of God teaches not the absence of fear? If you fear nothing, you will do whatever you want and not care about the outcome, even if it involves destruction to others. If you humble yourself in Love under the Word of God you will see the person executing judgement unrighteously, but you will understand your greater reward may not be in this present world as we know it, but in the after life.

Fear no man, but respect and honor him, only fear
the one that can destroy and send spirit, soul, and body
to eternal death.

God has placed a paradise in this earth for all man-kind to be satisfied, but man has not yet seen the paradise God has for him, because he reaches for the outward things in his life. Nevertheless, God knew pride with greed, and sexuality would stand in the way of man-kind receiving God's gifts in life, so he made a way for man to escape, if they choose to take it. **IT IS JESUS, THE SON OF GOD, WHO IS RICH IN GRACE AND MERCY, SLOW TO ANGER.**

**How are you responding to life situations?**

**ARE YOU APPLYING THE WORD OF GOD TO YOUR LIFE AND CONCERNING OTHERS.**

If there is unity in our spirit, soul and body there will always be Victory, if you **do not lose heart**.

May God bless and mature you in the spirit of our Lord
and Savior, Jesus Christ, so victory can be yours in the
battles you face in this life.

My prayer is that everyone who reads this book will have divine deliverance in whatever area in your life that is not representing the principles and standards spoken in the Word of God. May the Spirit of God strengthen your Heart in Love to over come the wiles created by man made deeds in this present world.

Understand this world has lost its glory. So, start a new life in Christ Jesus, receive His glory, understanding in your heart that you are a survivor, and will stay alive in the Spirit of God.

This book has been sent through the Spirit of Our Father in Heaven to give you a new direction in this present world!!!

- **With God, you can be the Best**
- **With God, you can soar like an Eagle**
- **With God, you can love Unconditionally**
- **With God, you can have Unspeakable Joy**
- **With God, no one can touch His love that dwells within your heart**
- **With God, you can go in Love and Peace and sin no more, In Jesus' Name**
- **With God, you can be an overcomer**
- **With God, you can be all he created you to be**
- **With God, you can love the unlovable, reach the unreachable, teach the unteachable**
- **For with God, nothing shall be impossible, Luke 1:37**

**IN JESUS NAME, AMEN!**

**A PROPHTESS VOICE TO BE HEARD IN THIS PRESENT WORLD**